DEAR
FATHER,
DEAR SON

TWO LIVES...
EIGHT HOURS

NEW YORK TIMES BESTSELLING AUTHOR
LARRY ELDER

 WND Books

DEAR FATHER, DEAR SON
WND Books
Washington, D.C.

Book Designed by Mark Karis

WND Books are distributed to the trade by:
Midpoint Trade Books
27 West 20th Street, Suite 1102
New York, NY 10011

WND Books are available at special discounts for bulk purchases. WND Books, Inc.
also publishes books in electronic formats. For more information call
(541-474-1776) or visit www.wndbooks.com.

First Edition

Hardcover ISBN: 978-1-936488-45-2
eBook ISBN: 978-1-936488-97-1

Library of Congress information available

Printed in the United States of America
10 9 8 7 6 5 4 3 2 1

TO RANDOLPH ELDER. THANK YOU.

CONTENTS

PART THREE: POSTSCRIPT

· PART ONE ·

EN ROUTE

"I DON'T ENJOY IT"

His face was hard. Not just his expression, but his skin. It, too, was hard—sandpaper hard.

When we were little kids, before the whippings started, we would jump in his lap when he came home from work. I would put my arms around his thick neck and hug him. But when I kissed his cheek, his skin was so rough it hurt my lips. "This must be why," I thought, "Mom never kisses Dad."

I'd never seen them kiss. Not a peck on the cheek. Not a pat on the behind. Not an air kiss. Not an accidental bump—even when they squeezed through the narrow aisles at Dad's restaurant. Not a smile or a hug or even a shrug from Mom when he walked in from work. They never held hands either.

When my older brother Kirk started shaving, the razor made his face bleed and break out into ugly pink and white bumps, mostly on his neck and under his chin. It embarrassed him so much that he made excuses to get out of going to school. No matter what kind of shaver he tried, the blade did something hideous to his skin. He finally discovered Magic Shave, a formulated-for-black-men chemical cream depilatory with a God-awful smell. Though it was time-consuming to mix the powder with water in an old coffee cup, carefully spread the paste on his face, and scrape it off with a butter knife, it worked. Kirk's skin slowly improved. But his face remained scarred for years.

"I don't have time for that mess," Dad said when Mom recommended Magic Shave.

Dad had had the same problem when he started shaving. His face erupted and scabbed. Still, every day he used the same razor, conquering the bumps by turning them into blisters, and the blisters, over the years, into a scratchy, dry leather. After each shave, he picked up a bottle of green aftershave, poured some in his hand, and splashed his face. Mom told us that the stuff stung like hell and burned his face. Dad never flinched.

"Ladies and Gentlemen, we are approaching the Los Angeles International Airport. The captain has switched on the 'fasten your seatbelt' sign."

I looked down from the plane at the soaring arches of the Theme Building at LAX. I smiled. My two brothers and I used to call it the "Jetsons's Building" because of the cartoon show about the happy, futuristic Jetson family with its hapless but loveable husband and father.

I remembered when Mom told us about the "rotating" restaurant at the top.

"Can we eat there?" we asked. "Please? Can we? Please?"

"Someday," she always said. "Someday." Someday meant never. Someday meant when horses quack. I know now that we simply couldn't afford to spend money on something so frivolous, but she would never say such a thing. Dad just said, "No. And don't ask again."

In a half-hour, counting the time to pick up luggage, I would be on my way to the diner.

I hated my father—really, really hated him. I hated working for him and hated being around him. I hated it when he walked through the front door at home. And we feared him from the moment he pulled up in front of the house in his car.

Back then, cars had "curb feelers," little coiled wires that stuck out from the wheel well or the bottom of the car on the passenger side, to tell parking drivers their distance from the curb. As soon as we heard the grinding sound of metal against cement, one of us would say, "He's home." Immediately everything changed. Everyone, including my mother, got quieter.

When Dad walked through the front door, he was usually scowling—a massive, dark hulk. He sat in his green lounge chair, "Dad's chair," where no one else was allowed to sit. My mother never even sat there. He opened the evening paper and often fell asleep, the paper spread across his chest. I would signal to my brothers, point at our father, and hold my index finger to my mouth.

"Shu-u-u-u-ush. He's asleep."

Kirk and Dennis nodded, and from three rambunctious kids, we turned into three little kittens tiptoeing around the junkyard dog as though there was a sign that read: "Guard Dog On Duty. Do Not Disturb."

One night, my little brother and I took a bath together. I was five. Dennis was fifteen months younger. We started a water fight—throwing, splashing, kicking, and ducking. The floor was soaked. Dirty bath water dripped from the ceiling and the walls. We laughed and started to wipe the water up when Dennis suddenly stopped and stared past me. I slowly turned around.

There stood Dad.

This time, he had the telephone cord. He grabbed me, held me dripping wet and naked in the air, and fired away. Dennis shook and waited his turn.

"Dad, please, no." He begged. "We were just playing, Dad. Dad, we'll clean it up! No! No! Please!"

The louder we hollered, the harder he swung. Our welts were visible for days.

My father, we always believed, punished us because he was angry, not because we'd done something bad, or at least bad enough to warrant punishment this severe. Dad just stomped around the house pissed off—a six-foot, 220-pound powder keg with a short and completely unpredictable fuse.

"I don't enjoy whippin' you," he said, finally putting down the telephone cord, watching us still shaking and whimpering. "No, I don't enjoy it at all."

NORMAL WAS HATE

"Pico Boulevard near Figueroa," I told the cab driver.

The place was Elder's Snack Bar at 1230 Valencia Street. My father somehow managed to start the tiny café sixteen years earlier with savings from the two jobs he worked as a janitor. He'd long talked about "bein' my own boss." He did it. He worked even longer hours. The pressure to make the café succeed made him even angrier and made us fear him even more.

Had it really been ten years? It was time. I needed to say something to him. I didn't care how he would react or what, if anything, he would say. What could he say? He treated us like shit. And I'd finally grown a pair and intended to tell him what a mean son-of-a-bitch he was.

My hatred for my father was not the kind where you do something bad, get a spanking, seethe for a bit, and then things go back to normal because, after all, you understand that he punishes you because he loves you. No, normal was intimidation. Normal was tense. Normal was not knowing whether you would say something that would set him off. And that could be anything. Normal was hate.

"Kirk! Larry! You stop that," Mom called from the window one evening.

We were "sword fighting," using branches off the big bush in the yard next door. We were pretending to be pirates and we weren't ready to stop. Dad wasn't home yet so we had a grace period before Mom got really mad.

"Boys! Put those things down! You're gonna put somebody's eye out!"

We kept playing.

"You two get in here this minute!" she hollered.

"When we're ready," Kirk said defiantly.

"Yeah," I said, raising the ante. "When we're good and ready."

What's the worst that can happen? We'll eventually come in. She'll spank us—she didn't hit very hard—and if we "cry" hard enough, she won't even tell Dad.

"When we're good and ready," Kirk repeated. "And don't ask again."

Suddenly that deep, angry voice slashed through the summer evening air.

"How dare you talk to your mother like that?" he shouted. "Now get your little black asses in here right now. I will . . . straighten . . . you . . . out!"

Dad! Jesus, how did he sneak home? What happened to the early warning from his curb feelers?

"I said, get in here right now! And I'm goin' to take care of you two! You think you're grown. I'll show you who's grown!"

Kirk looked at me. I looked at Kirk. He took off! I followed. We ran from the house, down the street, and around the corner, pumping as hard as we could.

"You come back here! You come back here right now!" Dad yelled. "If you know what's good for you, you'll get back here right now!"

By now, we had gone too far. We were committed. Dad charged out of the house and ran toward us. How could somebody that big and that old run that fast? But our lead was too big.

Now what? We had run away from home!

Kirk and I made plans. We would move to Huntsville and live on the farm where Mom grew up and talked about someday returning to live. But we didn't know where Huntsville was, had never been there before, and our parents wouldn't even let us cross the street. Wherever Huntsville was, we'd have to cross the street to get there. So Huntsville was out.

I knocked on a neighbor's door.

"Would you cook for me?" I asked the mother of a classmate. She told me she had her hands full taking care of her own family, and that I'd have better luck getting fed if I went back home.

"Can't," I said. "I ran away from home. My father is going to whip me."

She told me that running away wasn't the answer. Oh, no? Let her try getting whipped by my father.

I never dreamed I'd say the words, "I ran away from home." That's something other kids did. No one refused to obey my father. This was uncharted territory. I was afraid to keep running, but I was much more afraid to go home.

Kirk and I had now been gone for a good half hour. We kept circling the block, making plans for the future.

"Maybe we can keep walking until Dad goes to sleep, then gets up, and goes to work," I said. "And he'll forget the whole thing."

"Maybe I can be a lifeguard," Kirk said.

"Maybe I can dig for gold," I said.

But that seemed like a limited career choice, too. Not being able to cross the street was a huge problem because I had never seen any gold on our side. Nothing seemed workable, and to make matters worse, we were getting hungry. Maybe we should have eaten before we ran away.

We walked around another corner. Dad!

He'd leapt from behind a parked car. How did we not see him crouching down there? He ran at us. I ran as fast as I had ever run, but this time he quickly closed the gap. Kirk raced way ahead of me and got farther and farther away. I was alone.

As Dad's hand got closer, I had only one hope—I needed to cross the street.

I ran to the curb. But before I stepped off, he grabbed my t-shirt and jerked me back. Kirk was now a little bug running in the dark.

"Boy, I know you wasn't goin' in the street!"

I cried and told him I wasn't.

"Boy, don't you lie to me! You were goin' in the street, and don't tell me you wasn't."

The indictment had suddenly been amended to include not only running away, but attempted street crossing and perjury. Kirk kept running.

"Dad," I said, as he marched me back home. "Please don't whip me. You're right. I tried to cross the street."

I tried to bargain for a lesser sentence. Technically, I hadn't actually crossed it since he snatched me before I did.

"Please don't whip me."

He kept walking.

"I won't do it again."

Nothing.

I offered to go back and help with Kirk's capture.

Nothing.

"I know all his hiding places," I said.

Then I had an idea. Of course! Why hadn't I thought of it before?

"Dad, you know all the money I have in my piggy bank?"

Home, The Belt, and a massive whipping were just minutes away.

"If you don't whip me, I'll give it to you."

He stopped.

"Boy, you tryin' to bribe me?"

I didn't know what a bribe was, but gave myself a 50/50 shot of correctly answering the question.

"Yes," I said, "I'm trying to bribe you. And I have enough money to bribe Mom, too."

It was the hardest whipping I ever had.

Dad then got in his car and drove off to find the other fugitive—for Kirk had done the unthinkable. He had crossed the street. And once he crossed one street, he crossed several more. Was he on his way to Huntsville?

Dad found him several blocks away, and pulled in a driveway to block Kirk. My brother turned and ran the other way. Dad jumped out of the car, slamming the door shut so hard that the window shattered. He stopped, turned around, and looked at the broken glass. How much was that going to cost?

"Look at what you did!" he yelled at Kirk. "Dammit, look at what you did!"

"I'm dead," Kirk thought. No point in surrendering now. He kept running. Dad had never been this mad.

It was a good two hours before Dad caught him. Kirk was screaming when Dad, his shirt stuck to his back with sweat, hauled him into the house.

"Do you how many times this boy crossed the street?" Dad hollered to Mom.

He said he caught Kirk hiding behind a bush, but Kirk later told Dennis and me that he decided to turn himself in. "'Else," Kirk bragged like a defeated boxer who went the distance, "Dad wouldn't 'a caught me."

"This is all your fault!" I pointed at Kirk as Dad dragged him across the floor to the dresser, where he opened the top drawer and pulled out The Belt.

"Boy, shut up!" Dad said. "Would you jump off a bridge if your brother told you? Don't make me have to whip you again."

ON THE RECEIVING END

My father and I had not talked to each other since "That Friday" in the café. He didn't know I was in town. I didn't call him. This will be the first meaningful conversation with my father in ten years—unless you count, "How about those Rams?" "How about those Dodgers?" Or, "Is it still raining?" It had been a long, hard, cold war.

Watching the familiar streets outside the taxicab window, I thought about the night I went to jail. I never once thought about calling him to get me out. I knew that even before hearing my version of what happened, he would side with the cops and say that I got what I deserved for "mouthin' off."

"Why in God's name does anybody but a fool end up in jail?" I knew he would have said. "I've been on my own since I was thirteen and I've never been to jail. What's your excuse?"

It's funny now, three years later. But that night, it was as if Dad willed the arrest to humiliate me. Hell, one cop even accused me of the same thing—"mouthing off." And it didn't help that I had done just that. I was in Hollywood and I crossed the street against a blinking "don't walk" sign. Two cops stood on the corner. One used his index finger to tell me to approach him. He accused me of illegally crossing the street—a recurring theme in my life, apparently—and asked for ID.

"I don't have any ID," I said.

Question asked. Question answered. But did I stop there? No. This is what happens after two years of law school: "I'm a pedestrian," I told the cop. "I'm not operating a motor vehicle. This isn't the Soviet Union. I'm not required to have ID. Perhaps you and your partner should be concentrating on doing something about crime."

"Smartass, 'eh?" the officer said. "You're going to jail, motherfucker."

I was locked up for eight hours. When Mom asked where I was all night, I told her that I spent the night in jail.

"For what?"

I told her what happened.

"I see," she said. "You were mouthing off."

"Just don't tell Dad."

I'd flown in from Cleveland. I had settled there after law school, without running the decision by Dad. I hadn't lived in L.A. since I graduated from high school. The city felt less like home and more like someplace I used to know. But then, that's why I left, wasn't it, to find my own way away from him—away from the shouting, the rants, and the put-downs? I wanted to realize my potential and to do it without his advice, without his input, and without his guidance—not that he ever showed much interest in offering any.

I needed to talk to him.

He needed to know how I felt about how he treated us, and why his relationship with my brothers and me was either shitty or non-existent. He needed to hear a few things: what I needed as a child, where he fell way short, the kind of father I wanted—the kind I deserved but never had. If this pissed him off forever, so be it.

I was tired of being afraid of him, of holding so many things in, of letting him walk all over me. This was it. He needed to understand, Goddammit, that there was a fucking human being on the receiving end of his yelling, screaming, and cursing.

Family outings with Dad always deteriorated into an endurance test between Dad and my brothers and me. Thankfully, these outings were rare. Something always happened to upset him, and we'd end up leaving early.

At Disneyland, the first ride we hit was the Matterhorn rollercoaster. Dad twisted his neck and spent the rest of the day berating the theme park for his pain, complaining that he had to pay for the privilege of walking around with a "crooked" neck, arguing that the rollercoaster failed to post warnings, and noting that the designer of the Goddamn park "should be ashamed of himself."

"Dad, why don't we just go home?" asked my little brother, Dennis.

"What did you say?"

"Nothing."

Dad now shifted his wrath from Walt Disney to Dennis.

"What is that supposed to mean?"

"Well—"

"Shut up! I said, 'What is that supposed to mean?'"

"Well—"

"Shut up!"

Dennis stopped eating his cotton candy and tried not to cry. We didn't stay long.

My first Major League Baseball game was between the newly

transplanted Los Angeles Dodgers and the Milwaukee Braves at the L.A. Coliseum. A mysterious force made Dad buy tickets one row in front of a guy with a horn blaster—the kind that emits a sound only slightly less obnoxious than an ambulance siren. Dad wanted to kill the guy, but Mom threatened to leave if Dad "made a scene."

"Don't you say anything to that man," she warned. She said lots of people had those things.

"Who invented those Goddamn things?!" Dad said.

"This is a ballpark, not a church. If you don't want to cheer, you shoulda stayed home."

Instead, Dad spent the rest of our time in the ballpark attacking rude fans in a voice loud enough for the guy to hear. But the horn blower had heard my mother's admonishment and knew the troops were on his side, so he blasted away. We left in the sixth or seventh inning. I'm pretty sure Hank Aaron hit a home run. But all I really remember about that game are Dad, Dennis, and the man with the "Goddamn horn."

Dad took us to see the Fourth of July fireworks at a park with a big grassy area that served as a parking lot. It was stacked parking, where an attendant directs the driver to the next open spot in a line of multiple columns. So a driver parked in the interior must wait for another car to leave before there's enough room to pull out. Having no choice, Dad parked as directed—in the middle.

With the night sky still aglow from the fireworks finale, Dad hustled us toward the parking lot. "Gotta beat the traffic."

But we were the first in our stack to arrive. Maybe the first in the whole parking lot.

"Where the hell is everybody, Goddammit!"

Checkmated in the front and back and on either side, Dad fumed while waiting for others who were obviously taking "their own sweet time."

"Let's get in the car and wait. Might as well rest," Dad said.

He slumped down in his seat behind the wheel and covered his face with his hat. After a while, I decided to see if he was asleep. I lifted up the hat.

"Dammit! Why did you do that?" He acted as if he'd been poked in the ear with an ice pick.

"I was just check—"

"Shut up! Why'd you do that?"

"I was just—"

"Shut up! I work my ass off and all I ask is for a little bit of Goddamn sleep!"

Another long, silent ride home. It was the first and last family Fourth of July fireworks observance with Dad.

If he said he was going to do something, he did it. No back-and-forth. No half measures. No excuses.

He started smoking cigarettes at thirteen when he left home. One day, he complained about a scratch in his throat and went to see a doctor. In those days, even before warning labels on tobacco products, the doctor told my dad his cigarettes were "cancer sticks" and that they caused the scratchiness.

"I quit," he said.

He never smoked again. After almost thirty years of three packs a day, he just quit.

Mom, on the other hand, started smoking because of Dad. She used to light his cigarettes for him, and just picked it up from there.

Over the years, she tried to quit. She tried cold turkey. She tried gradually cutting down. She tried anti-smoking gum. She told us to hide her cigarettes, to throw out her cigarettes, and to charge her 10 cents every time she lit up. Nothing worked.

But Dad? "I quit"—and that was that. His willpower made

us fear him even more.

To save money, Dad bought some clippers and shears and began to cut our hair. Kids laughed at "the barber who picks at your head." They didn't know the barber they ridiculed was our dad. He butchered our hair. He had no regard for what was in style. And he took forever, which meant being in his presence, close up, every other Sunday, with the always-present chance for him to get mad at something we said or something we didn't say. Only after Kirk got into high school and rebelled did Dad stop cutting his hair. After Kirk spoke up, Dennis and I did, too. Dad hung up his clippers.

"All right, but don't you ask for a raise in your allowance," he said.

On Sunday nights, Dad watched the "Ed Sullivan Show."

"Kirk. Larry. Dennis. Come look!"

No matter what we were doing, we dropped everything, as Dad demanded, rushed to the television, and suffered through something he assumed we enjoyed—a ventriloquist, dueling jugglers, or the sequin-shirted guy running around keeping plates spinning at the end of long sticks, including one in each hand and one in his mouth.

"Look at that," he'd say.

"Wow, Dad." We faked interest, drummed our fingers on the floor, and counted down the seconds until the act ended and we could return to our little zone of freedom—somewhere away from him in another part of the house.

None of us dared say, "You know, Dad, I really don't give a rip about Topo Gigio and his stupid little puppet friends. Or Sonny Liston jumping rope. Or Kate Smith singing 'God Bless America.' Really, Dad."

One night, Dennis and I were polishing our shoes for Sunday services the next morning, and Dennis starting singing a song that was sweeping the playground in third grade. It was a stupid song, of all things, about a popular brand of chocolate syrup:

I hate Bosco.
It's not good for me.
My mother puts it in my milk
To try to poison me.
But I fooled my mother.
I put it in her tea.
And now there's no more mother
To try to poison me.

Dad exploded.

"What are you doin' singin' a song about murderin' your mother?!"

"Dad, it's just a s—"

"I don't give a damn. I don't want to hear it again."

"But Dad, Mom never said anything—"

"It's not up for debate, dammit!"

Even on Christmas Day, we felt tension. One Christmas, the drama started a couple of days early. Dad kept up the fiction that Santa Claus brought us our gifts. Our house had no fireplace, the doors were always locked, and some of our friends lived in apartments. The logistics of getting gifts to every kid, on time, no matter where they lived, had long ago stopped adding up. Anxious to see what my parents were getting me, I went into their closet, which was always off-limits. An air rifle! Just what I wanted.

After he came home from work, I bragged about my detective work.

"I know what Santa Claus is getting me for Christmas."

"Oh, yeah? What?" he said from behind the evening paper.

"An air rifle."

"Goddammit! Who said you could go through my closet?!

Who?!"

"No one, I—"

"Now you've ruined Christmas, Goddammit! Go to your room!"

I wasn't sure if it was because I busted his Santa Claus myth, or that I had spoiled Christmas since the gift was no longer a surprise, but after that, I never really enjoyed the air rifle.

Even on Christmas, Mom and Dad showed no affection toward each other.

New kitchenware. "Thanks, Randolph."

New, fluffy, terry-cloth robe. "Thanks, Vi."

Perfume. "Thanks, Randolph."

The Christmas event Dad enjoyed the most was finding a package that was tightly bound with string, or a box that someone struggled to open. My Aunt Juanita from Chattanooga always sent pajamas in boxes that were securely wrapped with thick string.

"I'll get that," Dad said, as we tugged and pulled on the strings. "Hand it to me."

He stood up, reached into his pocket, and pulled out this bulky red tool—a Swiss Army knife. Dad carried it with him every day of the year, but Christmas Day was the only time I ever saw him use it. He carefully selected the appropriate blade and slowly sawed through the string.

"There." Triumphant, he handed the package back. "Anybody else? No?"

Back into his pocket went the knife, where it would remain for another 364 days.

· 4 ·

"I'LL GIVE YOU SOMETHING TO CRY ABOUT"

L.A. traffic. You never quite get used to it. While the driver cut down side streets to outmaneuver the congestion, I thought about what led up to That Friday—reliving it again and again.

I was fifteen and had worked for him three straight summers and on Saturdays year-round when, for a while, the restaurant was open six days a week. And I despised every minute of it. That Friday, that moment, that time, I just wasn't going to take it or him anymore.

At the restaurant, when things got busy during "rush hour," from about 11:30 until 2 p.m., he cooked furiously, sweat like crazy, and barked out orders like a boot camp sergeant.

"Get this. Get that. Dammit, I thought I told you—"

Do the wrong thing and the cursing would start, and it didn't matter if customers heard it.

I hated the restaurant. It was a diner, really. Fifteen stools placed a few inches apart and set up in a "U" shape so that every customer faced the grill, where my father presided. My parents could never even decide on what to call Elder's Snack Bar. The café. The restaurant. The snack bar. Mostly they called it "the place." Dad worked seven days a week, even though the restaurant eventually closed on weekends. On Saturdays, he still got up early.

"It's the only day I can get away to get supplies," he said.

On Sundays, he needed to "set up the week," and was gone almost all day. My brothers and I didn't care. He probably didn't want to be home any more than we wanted him there. Whenever he was around, the weather was cloudy with a chance of thunderstorms.

"Your father is going to build a restaurant," my mother announced a couple of years before it opened. I visualized a big, darkly lit ballroom with tables and chairs, a hostess, and maybe a piano—like in a Shirley Temple movie, where people get dressed up, pull up in big cars, and hand their keys to a valet. A restaurant! We're building a restaurant!

The glass and aluminum shoebox building was hot, with small narrow aisles barely wide enough for one person to walk through without turning sideways. I was ten when he opened the restaurant. At first, I washed dishes, mopped the floor, squeegeed the windows, and cleaned the toilet. I wanted to wait on customers like Kirk so I could earn tips. But Dad wouldn't hear of it.

"I don't like kids handlin' food," he said.

"But—"

"It's not up for discussion."

Dad was a former Marine, and working for him was like being in the military—everything done on time, at the same time, no excuses.

"Larry, it's time," Dad said, when he woke me up at 4:30 a.m. No snooze button. I had five minutes to get ready.

By 4:35, we were in the car. The restaurant opened at 6:30, giving us one hour and fifty-five minutes to cram everything in. We drove through streets, still dark and empty, to pick up supplies. We got to the restaurant at 5:10. I took down the stools that I'd sat upside-down on the counter the night before. I wiped off the counter and the stool seats. Then I stood at attention, ready to fetch whatever he needed.

Cups?

"Right."

Potatoes?

"Right."

Cooking grease. Paper place mats. Sugar. Napkins. Jelly in the glass containers. Refill the salt and pepper shakers. Straws. Plastic baskets for the French fries.

He barked out three or four things to do, and God help me if I did them out of order—and the proper order wasn't necessarily the order in which he gave them.

"Prioritize, dammit," he said, when I once asked which task he wanted done first.

"You mean, read your fucking mind," I said to myself.

"I thought I told you to fill those catsup bottles." He hadn't.

"Why isn't the coffee machine on?" It was.

"Who told you to put out so much bacon?" He had.

"Why didn't you bring out an order tablet when you were in the back?" I had. It was under the newspaper that he had set right on top of it.

At 6:10, Dad turned on the grill and the deep fry, and took out the eggs, bacon, and ham. He chopped up onions, grated cheese, and boiled potatoes to make hash browns. He took out scales with weights and measures. Like a chemist, he used the precise amounts of flour, salt, and sugar for the pancake mix and the biscuit dough. Everything was fresh and homemade—biscuits, pancake mix, pecan and apple and sweet potato and cherry pies, and German chocolate cake. The menu, for such a small place, was gigantic. My mother wanted him to pare down the number of offerings. Dad refused. He liked making so many different things. He considered himself an artist. A customer once called the diner a "fast-food" place.

"Fast food?" Dad was insulted. "Fast food? You think you can get this at McDonalds? Fast food!?"

As much as I hated it, Dad loved the restaurant. He loved working for himself. And he loved cooking. More than that, he loved performing. He didn't know it, but when he cooked—juggling so many different orders—he had a slight smile. It said, "That's right. I'm good. We both know it." There was absolutely no wasted motion.

He was a music conductor in front of his five-foot-by-three-foot grill, the stovetop at stage right. In his hand, instead of a baton, was a spatula. Denver omelet, upper right corner—the woodwinds. Hash browns, middle right side—the brass. Omelet, no ham, middle rear—tympani. Pancakes, to the left—piano. Grits, in the pot on the stove—the bass. Eggs, over easy, in the front—the strings. Now all together!

He flipped the eggs a good foot and a half or more above the pan, never missing a landing and never breaking a yolk. He carefully rolled up the omelet. When the toast popped up, he dipped a small brush in the melted butter, stroked each piece, and cut them diagonally. Without looking, he grabbed a plate from overhead. He placed the eggs, hash browns, and toast in exactly the same spot every time. A customer once shook her head at the sight and said, "Jesus, Randy, you're like a surgeon."

The bastard was good.

Back at home, the three of us kids drove Mom crazy. Our first house—the one where I lived until I was seven, the one my father knocked down to build the café—had no backyard. Kirk was three-and-a-half years older than me, and Dennis, called—what else—"Dennis the Menace," was fifteen months younger.

We were like three hamsters trapped in a shoebox-sized cage, jockeying for the same spinning wheel. We shared a tiny bedroom. Kirk had his own bed, and Dennis and I slept in bunk beds with Dennis up top. My father determined this arrangement.

"Wait 'til your father comes home," my mother said, when we "acted out." And we acted out a lot.

She insisted we speak "proper English," and would correct our grammar anywhere, anytime, on the spot.

"Can you bring a candy bar for me and Dennis?"

"I can, if it's 'for Dennis and me.'"

Kirk didn't make up his bed. Dennis played with his food. I wouldn't eat mine. We lost a toy. We found a toy. Dennis claimed the toy was his. Dennis traded his wagon for a broken tricycle I no longer used. Then he wanted his wagon back.

"No. A deal's a deal."

"No, it's not."

"Yes, it is."

"Larry, give Dennis his wagon back."

"No."

"Fine, wait 'til your father comes home."

"Told you," Dennis said.

"Wait 'til your father comes home" usually meant Dennis and I got into a fight. A real fight—a fist fight. And we fought every single day, several times a day, seven days a week. We couldn't stand each other. His temper was like my Dad's, and this made me dislike my little brother even more. Even though Dennis and I knew we'd "get a whippin'" for "actin' out," we still fought.

"Wait 'til your father comes home."

He treated infractions like misdemeanors, misdemeanors like felonies, and felonies like capital offenses. He'd go to the dresser, open up the top drawer, and pull out The Belt—a tightly coiled, shiny, brownish-orange "crocodile" belt. I didn't know if it was real crocodile. Kirk said it was.

With a short flick, Dad would uncoil it, fold it in half, and crack it.

"All right, dammit, I've had just about enough."

Once I said, "Why don't you wait until you've had all of about enough?" Kirk laughed.

Dad whipped us both extra hard. I never said it again.

"I'll whip you until I get tired," he'd say. Or, "Boy, if you don't stop cryin', I'll give you somethin' to cry about."

When the crying continued, he said, "All right. If you know what's good for you, you'll stop."

I guess it didn't occur to him that if I could stop crying and put a stop to the whole thing, I would. And that if he'd stop whipping me, I'd stop crying.

"Oh, so you think you're grown," he sometimes said, as he cracked The Belt.

Sometimes he came home a little earlier than usual. To his chair he went.

"Where's the *TV Guide*?"

The magazine arrived each week in the mail. By Wednesday or Thursday, it could be anywhere. Dad wanted it right there, on the little stand next to his chair. When he reached for it, he expected to find it. And it damn well better be there.

"I said, where is the *TV Guide*?"

Whatever we were doing, it was now all hands on deck.

"Dammit, where . . . is . . . the . . . damn . . . *TV Guide*?"

"Here it is!" One of us would say, out of breath, after having retrieved it from beneath a stack of comic books under the bunk beds. "It's right here, Dad."

Disaster averted. As you were.

Once, Dad pretended to be angry. Dennis and I were arguing, except we were more quiet about it than usual because Dad was in his chair in the living room. But he hit the ceiling.

"I told you to cut out all that noise!" He got up and walked to the dresser and opened the top drawer. By now, Dennis and I were shaking and crying—and a little bewildered. We weren't that loud, were we, even for him?

"C'mon you two," he said, then closing the drawer without retrieving The Belt.

"I was just kiddin'." He laughed and sat back down.

Our reaction should have made him re-think his whole approach to discipline, and realize that there's something deeply wrong when a joke causes that kind of sheer panic. But it didn't.

I decided to do something about it. The Belt had to go. I told Dennis, and he advised me not to do it.

"Don't try and stop me." He didn't. That made him a co-conspirator and therefore unlikely to tell on me. So far, so good.

"I'm going to get rid of it," I said. "And you better not tell."

Kirk, under pressure, might fold. So I didn't bring him in. I waited until Kirk was not home. Mom was in the kitchen. I went into Dad and Mom's bedroom with a phonebook in either hand. I put them on the floor in front of the dresser, stepped on the books, grabbed a knob in each hand, and pulled. The drawer wouldn't budge. I pulled harder. The right side of the drawer slowly opened, but the left side barely moved. I pushed the right side back and started over. Pop! I stopped and waited. Had the noise alerted Mom? Now I knew I needed to pull both sides with equal force. Too hard, and the drawer might come out, spilling everything onto the floor. Too soft and it wouldn't open.

"Wait 'til your father gets home!" I could just hear Mom's famous words if I failed.

Carefully, I tugged again, and tried to evenly pull both sides of the drawer. It balked, but with each tug, the drawer came out a little more. I saw cuff links, tiepins, pens, coins, and a lot of little boxes. But there, in the lower left-hand corner, I saw it. The Belt. I grabbed it up, pushed the drawer shut, picked up the phone books, and left. Mom was still in the kitchen.

Now where to put it? In front of our house was a big curbside sewer opening. When it rained, dirty water flowed in and drained down, en route to who knows where. Perfect. I threw The Belt down the hole. Dad had been disarmed.

When Mom punished us, it was almost like being sent to summer camp.

We'd do something silly and she'd say, "Stop playing with your food. John Lesley knows better than that."

When she found strings of bubblegum stuck to the bed sheet, "Dennis, you fell asleep with gum in your mouth. John Lesley knows better than that."

"Who's John Lesley?" I once asked.

"He's the village idiot."

"What's a 'village idiot'?"

"Never mind. Go polish your shoes."

When she really got angry, she'd "whip us."

"Go get me a switch."

She sent us out in the yard, and told us to break a thin branch from a nearby tree. She waved it around like Zorro.

"It's too thin. Bring me another."

Outside we'd go, break off a thicker one, and bring it for her approval.

"This'll do."

Then she whacked us until we cried. It almost never hurt, and we'd wait until she gave us a reasonable amount of whacks before we "cried." Once we cried, she stopped.

Dad worked fiendishly hard. He left earlier than anybody's father on the block and came home later. On Sundays, he came home just a little earlier. Though he never went to church, my mother made us go every week, and she even taught Bible school. But Dad never went. Mom never asked him, and we didn't want him coming anyway. There was no telling what would set him off on the way there.

He seemed to resent us for being alive, for having to be fed, housed, and clothed. There was always tension between Mom and Dad, as if a low-grade siren or alarm was constantly going off. And much of it was about "the kids"—what we'd done, what we wanted, and whether they could afford it.

They never went out, not even to dinner. Even when my brothers and I were little, they never went anywhere together unless we went, too. The last time I saw them go anywhere together— without us—it had something to do with taxes or insurance.

We never had a party, even a small one, at our house—not even a friend over for the Super Bowl. Her friends never stayed for dinner—lunch, sure, but not dinner. And he had no friends. They stopped sleeping in the same bed so long ago, I can't recall the decade. And when I went away to college and created a vacant bedroom, they stopped sleeping in the same room.

Yes, "normal" was hatred and anxiety and fear and dread. Kirk, Dennis, and I never discussed our feelings about Dad. We didn't have to. I knew how they felt. They knew how I felt. When we were even younger, before a getting a whipping, we had tried running and crying to our mother in the hopes that she'd intervene. That just made him even angrier. So running was out of the question. By running to another room, you just wrote yourself a check for a longer and harder whipping.

From the time he said, "I've had just about enough," to the time he cracked the belt, you stood and waited. If he was whipping all three of us, he started with Kirk. Though Dad whipped us hard, Kirk did not cry easily. I watched him twist and struggle and snake to avoid the lashes while trying not to cry. Eventually he cracked. Then it was my turn. If you cried "too soon," he kept going. If you fought the tears, he assumed he wasn't hitting hard enough. No strategy really worked. Dad just wailed as long as he felt like it, depending upon his mood. Dennis was last, standing, watching, and trembling through two whippings before his turn. It wasn't exactly like storming the beach at Normandy when everybody ahead of you had been cut down by enemy fire. But to little kids, it was close.

Not long after I ditched The Belt, Dennis and I got into one of our fights.

"Stop it," Mom said.

"I said, 'Stop it.'"

"I'm not going to tell you again. Stop it."

"That's it. I'm going to tell your father."

She did.

"Dammit, I work and work to keep a roof over your head, food on the table, the lights on, and I come home and have to put up with this!"

He walked to the dresser, opened the drawer and—nothing. He opened the drawer underneath. I hadn't thought to look there!

"Where . . . is . . . the . . . belt?"

Dennis and I looked at each other.

"Dammit, where . . . is . . . the . . . belt?"

Dad closed the drawer and unbuckled the belt he was wearing. Zip! He folded it in half and whipped us. It hurt just as much as the crocodile. I don't think he ever suspected that one of us would have the cashews to take his belt.

It wasn't just whippings. He blew up in different and unpredictable ways.

"Pick up your stuff," Kirk told Dennis. "Dad's home."

"Get your stuff, Larry, or you know what's gonna happen," Kirk warned me.

Too late. I picked up my Slinky and most of my other toys. Dennis gathered up his marbles and some parts of his Erector set. But my toy dump truck—the red one I got for Christmas—was right in the middle of the living room, directly in his path.

Dad came in, walked right toward the truck, and wham! He kicked it like a punter going for a field goal. It smashed against the wall and shattered into big red plastic chunks.

"What'd I tell you about those damn toys!" he said, as he sat in his chair and opened the paper. "Next time you'll know better." He had destroyed a toy that he got me for Christmas because it was in the middle of the room.

Dad could smile. And sometimes did. When he smiled, he lit up like a big neon sign. He had a big, deep southern laugh that came from deep down in his hometown, Athens, Georgia. I could count on two hands the number of times he laughed—I mean really laughed—not the fake one he used when my mother thought something was funny but he didn't.

He was a walking volcano, always on the verge of erupting—and on its own schedule. No reason was too trivial. Sometimes he'd explode over something said or something done—the same something that he completely ignored at another time.

Take the time we were in the car and Dennis said he needed to use the bathroom.

"Boy, didn't I tell you to empty it out before we left the house? Dammit!" Dad yelled. "Now I have to find a fillin' station. Why didn't you listen?!"

The rubber ball Dad bought Kirk rolled into the sewer. Kirk said nothing about it.

"Where's that ball I gave you?" Dad asked three days later. "Why'd you stopped playin' with it?"

Kirk told him what happened, and Dad screamed at him.

"You boys can't keep nothin'!"

For crying out loud. All balls get lost, don't they? That's what balls do. They get lost. This wasn't the first time one of us lost a ball. The last time, Dad just shrugged and bought another one.

"Do you know how much that ball cost, dammit?"

When I wouldn't eat my lima beans or the egg yolk or the boiled potato, my mother complained but I was able to excuse myself from the table.

"Dammit," Dad sometimes said. "You're just gonna sit there until you get hungry!"

One time he made me sit for a couple of hours until I force-swallowed the Brussels sprouts.

"Boy, do you know how much food costs?!"

Dad took us to a drive-in movie every few months. We preferred a movie theater where we could sit away from him, and where he couldn't raise his voice. But the movie *The Fly* killed the theater outings.

In the film, a guy became a little fly with a human head.

"Help me! Help me!" he cried.

Dennis excused himself to go to the bathroom. Five minutes, ten, twenty—and still no Dennis. Dad went looking for him, and found him shivering on a couch in the corner of the lobby. The movie scared him to death.

"Goddammit, I work my behind off to pay for us to see a movie and you sit out in the lobby! I thought somebody kid-napped you!"

We left before the movie ended, and Dad yelled all the way home.

The Century Drive-In was the first in Los Angeles with a

giant, curving "Cinerama" wide screen. The new technology fascinated Dad, but to us it just meant spending several unpleasant hours closed inside a car with a human hand grenade. My brothers and I dreaded the whole ordeal. Our friends loved going to the movies, even to stupid Disney movies chosen by their parents. But with Dad, sooner or later, someone would say the wrong thing, do the wrong thing, or do the right thing in the wrong way—and the evening was spoiled. I'd rather have stayed home, but it wasn't like we got to vote.

One time, Dad sent Dennis to the snack bar to get popcorn. He made me go with him to make sure Dennis found his way back, because the last time Dennis went alone he didn't come back for almost forty-five minutes, and then only because Dad sent Kirk to find him. Dad's yelling and Dennis's crying spoiled the rest of the movie.

"Shut up," Dad said, "or I'll give you somethin' to cry about." So for the next hour-and-a-half, we all sat half-watching *The Parent Trap*—Dennis trying not to cry, Kirk and me angry at Dad for being so rough on Dennis, and my mother saying nothing. Just once, I wanted her to gently intercede like June Cleaver: "Randy, Dennis didn't get lost on purpose. Let's not ruin the evening for everybody."

Another time, Dad sent the three of us to get a big pizza with extra cheese.

"Don't turn the box upside down," he warned.

At the Art Deco–style snack bar, Dennis insisted on carrying the pizza.

"Remember what Dad said," Kirk reminded him.

"I'm not stupid."

So back to the car we went. I carried the drinks, Kirk the popcorn, and Dennis the pizza—which he promptly turned upside down. When Dad tried to open the box, the cheese stretched tightly from the pizza to the top of the box and the top practically snapped back. My mother laughed which, Kirk and I thought, might give us permission to laugh. But we thought better of it. Good move, because Dad went nuts.

"Dammit, I work all week, and I ask you to do one damn thing right."

· 5 ·

THE TEMPTATIONS

Traffic was better now. I looked at my watch. Fifteen minutes more.

God, his temper. The anger. The unpredictability. So fucking ridiculous. And he needed to know. Whether he was ready or not—he was going to hear it.

Dad never really knew—or cared—about how working at the restaurant left little time for me to do things with my friends like everybody else did. Friday was a big going out night. Everybody went out, but I had to work the next day and getting up at 4:30 a.m. meant going to bed at 9 p.m.

When I got home on Saturday, after working all day in the restaurant, I was exhausted and rarely went out.

"Be thankful you have a job, dammit," he said. "When I was your age, I had to hustle. You don't have to."

I just wanted one Saturday off.

The big thing on weekends was the Sportsman Park's Hunter Hancock Record Hop, a big bash about once every two months sponsored by radio station KGFJ. Because I worked, I never went. But I heard about it in school the next Monday. Friends said over a thousand kids came.

Just once before I died, I wanted to go. The popular Hunter Hancock was a white man who spun records at a black station. Everybody loved him. And he knew what we liked.

"All right everybody, let's go hunting wi-i-i-i-ith Hunter." And then he played the latest song from Brenton Woods or Little Anthony and the Imperials or Dobie Gray's hit, "The In Crowd."

"What, I'm supposed to cook and serve at the same time?" Dad said, whenever I asked for a Saturday off. "How many hands do you think I have?"

"Well, like most upper primates—" Or, "Unless you got one or two growing out of someplace I can't see and would rather not know about, I'd have to say two." But those responses only played in my head—I never said those things.

"Sure, take off, dammit, and how are we goin' to pay the house note?" he said.

"If my taking one day off means we lose the house, maybe we're over-leveraged." I never said those words, either.

"Why don't I just close the place down and work for somebody else?" he said.

"Well, with your attitude, Dad, I'd pretty much say you're darn near unemployable." And, of course, I never said that.

KGFJ was the "black" station that played R&B music—the Four Tops, The Supremes, Smokey Robinson & The Miracles, Marvin Gaye, The Contours, The Impressions, Mel Carter, Gladys Knight and The Pips, Gene Chandler, Hugh Masekela, The 5th Dimension, Mary Wells, The Toys, Aretha Franklin, Sam Cooke, and Jackie Wilson.

Kirk, at first, listened to KRLA and the other top 40 stations that played Elvis, the Beach Boys, Bobby Vee, Bobby Rydell, Shelley Fabres, and Ricky Nelson. Kirk was a big Elvis fan, the only self-admitted one any of us knew. Elvis wasn't cool in my neighborhood or at school. And KGFJ didn't play Elvis. Kirk didn't care. He played Elvis's records all the time on the little portable phonograph at home.

He went—and dragged Dennis and me—to all of The King's movies, from *Love Me Tender* to *King Creole* to the ones that even Kirk admitted were awful: *Double Trouble, Roustabout,* and *It Happened at the World's Fair.*

My mother let Kirk choose the movies; Dennis and I had no say. She gave us each 25 cents, plus 15 cents for popcorn, and it was off to *Blue Hawaii.*

Finally, even Kirk couldn't resist The Temptations, and switched to KGFJ, Hunter Hancock's station.

In the restaurant, Dad played "background" music. He wouldn't play KGFJ.

"It offends the customers," he said.

"How?"

"It's black music. We have black and white and Mexican customers. I don't want just black music. I ain't servin' soul food. We ain't playin' black music."

So he played the station that ran instrumental versions of "Moon River" or "Lazy, Hazy Days of Summer" or "Love is a Many Splendored Thing." Nobody was offended because nobody listened.

Dad did allow us listen to KGFJ in the car—finally. For a long time, Dad played the same station he played in the restaurant. But Kirk rebelled and insisted on KGFJ. Dad backed down, but only after Mom joined our side. I hoped that once Dad started listening to Motown, he'd actually enjoy it and play it at the restaurant. It might make things there just a little more bearable.

"Dad, listen to this," I said when the family was in the car.

"Who's that singin'?" he asked.

"Smokey Robinson," I said, "lead singer for The Miracles. He writes all their songs and stuff for the Temptations, too." Dad seemed genuinely interested.

"Huumph," my mother said. "Sounds like a girl." And she switched the channel.

I hatched a plan to go to the Hunter Hancock record hop. I'd get sick. On Monday I began sniffing and coughing.

"You okay?" Dad said.

"Yeah, I'm fine."

"You sure?"

"Yeah."

I dragged around, "toughing it out" until Thursday.

"You don't look good, maybe you should stay home tomorrow."

"You think so, Dad?"

"No need in you coughin' up 'round the customers. I'll get one of the girls to come in. Late notice. Have to pay overtime, dammit."

"You sure?"

Dad never got tired. There was no such thing as fatigue. He never got sick. Didn't believe in it. Weak people got sick—or got sick and weren't strong enough to keep it to themselves.

"Yeah," he sighed. "Stay home. Don't want you coughin' up on the customers."

After an afternoon of clock watching, Friday evening finally came. What to wear, what to wear? No, not those pants. This shirt with the big flyaway collar. I'll put in a tiepin in the left collar. At last. My first record hop. Solid!

To celebrate, I decided to smoke a whole cigarette. I had begun building up tolerance by sneaking Mom's Pall Malls and going behind the garage to practice. Little by little, I overcame the light-headedness, and could now smoke up to a half of a cigarette.

I learned to inhale and slowly blow out the smoke, like Bogart did in the movies, without getting dizzy.

I ran bath water, and wet a couple of towels and stuck them in the crack under the door to block out the smoke smell. I soaked in the hot water, lit the cigarette, and for the first time smoked a whole one, making little "O's" with the exhale. Wonder if I'll get a phone number tonight. Maybe two. The goal will be at least one.

Everything started spinning.

I got weak and dizzy. I climbed out of the tub and grabbed the doorknob to keep from falling. I crawled to the toilet and started throwing up. Mom banged on the door.

"What's going on? Are you all right?"

"Nothing."

"What do you mean nothing? You're throwing up."

"No, I'm not."

"Yes you are. Let me in there right now."

"Mom, I'm okay. I just don't feel well." I threw up again before I made it to bed. I wanted to lie down for a just few minutes to clear my head.

I woke up at 4 a.m. Three hours after the record hop ended.

Sunday morning I heard Dad talking to Mom, as she got ready for church.

"How's Larry?" he asked.

"He was throwing up Friday night. Spent Saturday morning in bed."

"Good thing I gave him the day off. Boy was sick."

6

"DON'T LET THE DOOR HIT YOU IN THE ASS"

Now the cab was minutes away from the restaurant. I was nervous and scared. It angered me that he still made me feel this way. But he was going to sit and, for the first time, listen to what I had to say. One more time, I went over That Friday—and what led up to it.

Mom and Dad never really argued. If they did, it wasn't in front of us. I never thought this was unusual until I met Steve Johnson. Steve and I were in the second grade. We both loved comic books, dismissively referred to by our parents as "funny books." We first read D.C., Superman and Batman, and then, like all alert and aware comic readers, we graduated to Marvel.

Steve's mother was as beautiful as any Hollywood actress. She had long, thick, shiny blonde hair that she constantly combed while smoking a cigarette. His father was a tall dark man with a "process"—hair that had been treated to straighten it.

The Johnsons were the only black-white couple in our neighborhood or, for all I knew, in the whole school district. Kids lowered their voices and stared at Mrs. Johnson when she walked Steve to school.

My mother said Mrs. Johnson's family was so incensed over the marriage that they stopped talking to her. And Mr. Johnson, according to Mom, "hated the world" because he tried to make a career as a singer, but failed. Steve once told me that his dad was a singer, and played a demo Mr. Johnson recorded years ago. I thought he was mediocre, but didn't tell Steve.

"Mr. Johnson is a prop builder at one of the studios. Hates it," Mom said.

She told me that the Johnsons were constantly in "money trouble"—even to the point of having their water and electricity shut off. Steve said that his dad once cooked their meals for a full week over a small outdoor barbeque grill. Steve tried to make it sound like an adventure, like camping. But that week he managed to stay long enough at my house three different times so that my mother invited him to stay for dinner.

"Oh, Mrs. Elder, I don't know. I've already eaten here twice this week." Soon he was helping himself to seconds.

The first time I visited his house, I saw dishes everywhere, even in the bedroom Steve shared with his brother. I saw cock-roaches—in the daytime. The drapes were torn. And the family drank out of Flintstone "glasses," which were really grocery store grape jelly jars with Fred and Wilma on the sides.

Steve and I were sitting on his bedroom floor reading.

"Fuck, Lillie, where are my mother-fucking pants?!"

Mrs. Johnson fired back.

"Look in the Goddamn closet, you fucking moron! And don't step on my Goddamn brush. Pick it up and hand it to me before you manage to lose that, too!"

This went on for several minutes. There were two other chil-dren in the house, Steve's older sister and little brother.

I looked up at Steve. He stared at his comic book and slowly turned a page.

"Are they always like this?" I started to ask. But Steve's reaction had already answered the question. His parents spoke like this all the time, not caring who heard.

My father is an ogre all right, but at least I'd never heard him say "fuck" or "shit" or "fuck you"—all of which I'd heard just in the last five minutes at Steve's house.

"Your parents aren't like that, are they?" he finally said.

"No, they're not."

"Didn't think so." He went back to Spiderman.

Mrs. Johnson invited me to stay for dinner. I thought about the cockroaches.

"No thank you, my mother made dinner."

"Ha!" she said. "Bet you're afraid of my bugs."

I jumped on my bike and rode home. And I couldn't wait to get there. "At least," I thought, "my house isn't like that."

Then came the restaurant.

I never saw my parents argue or even raise their voices to each other—until the restaurant. They worked together for about two years. My father knew exactly how the restaurant should be run, and so did Mom. They had two entirely different and contrasting visions. To Dad, it was a restaurant. To Mom, it was a breakfast and lunch stand. Dad wanted a large menu with homemade cakes and pies. Mom wanted it simple and streamlined.

They disagreed on the portions, the price, and whether coffee should be refilled for free. They quarreled over the name, the signage, and the tableware. Disagreement turned into argument, which turned into shouting. At first, the quarrels took place at the restaurant.

"Look at what we sell and eliminate the rest," she'd say.

"Let's cook things they can't get at fast-food places. That's our advantage," he'd counter.

Mom came home each evening with some new tale of verbal

abuse committed by Dad.

"Your father can't stand it when people compliment my Denver omelets," she said.

"Your father shouted at me, in front of a customer, just because he couldn't find the hot dog tongs."

"One more time! One more time! If he talks to me that way one . . . more . . . time, I'm leaving!"

"Your father ordered way too many potatoes for the week and when I told him, he didn't want to admit he was wrong. So a whole bag of potatoes spoiled."

Mom came home every evening and acted out for us the day's arguments. She complained about how he treated her. My hostility now broke the meter. It was no longer just about how he treated us, but about how he treated her.

"I was sick for one day—had a fever with chills. And he accused me of 'just trying to get out of work!'"

"He said 'Goddammit' to me in front of the coffee delivery man. I'll be damned if I'm going to put up with it."

"I told your father that if he talked to me that way one more time, I'm gone. You know what he said? Do you know what your father said? He said, 'Don't let the door hit you in the ass.'"

After this threat, she said he stopped yelling for a day, a week, or a month. Then it started up again. At first, he cursed at her in private, in the back. Then he did it in front of delivery people, then in front of the customers.

"He won't give me any credit for anything. I don't do anything right."

"If it weren't for me, the restaurant would be a failure," she said. "But your father thinks he's running the most successful business since General Motors."

"I ought to leave and show his stubborn black ass how much he needs me. And when he asks me to come back, I'll have found me a better job and he can just go to hell!"

Dad wanted to be the chief cook. Mom wanted to be the chief cook. Mom didn't like the way he prepared an omelet. Dad didn't like the way she prepared an omelet. Mom thought Dad was showing off when he tossed the eggs up the air and flipped them. Dad thought she couldn't do it because she didn't have the skill.

I wondered how many customers stopped coming because they couldn't digest their food while watching the wrestling match.

They disagreed about when the restaurant should open, when it should close, and whether it should stay open on weekends.

And in this increasingly Latino neighborhood, they disagreed about illegal immigration. And this was decades before the topic became a national lightening rod.

"They're taking over this country," she said. "Our schools. Hospitals. What other country lets people just walk across the border and help themselves? This is going to ruin this state."

A nervous paint-splattered Mexican man came in one day, and struggled to order a hamburger. He tried say what he wanted on it.

"Speak up." Mom said.

"Quiero—"

"Quiero, nothing, this is America."

"Quiero—"

"Quiero, nada. Speak English."

The man pointed.

"Pickles. You want pickles?" She held up a pickle. "Pick-el. Pick-el."

The man turned and left. Dad exploded.

"How would you like to be treated like that!?"

"I'm not in somebody else's country expecting them to speak

my language!"

"No, but you're running a Goddamn business."

"He should Goddamn learn English before walking into somebody's business and expecting service."

"We're not the border patrol! I want everybody's money."

"He's in America now. He better learn to say pickle!"

"He's a payin' customer!"

"He's not in Tijuana!"

"Dammit, Vi—"

"Dammit, Randolph."

And so it went, for two years, Monday through Friday. Mom came home and told us about that day's abuse, in great detail. Dad came home, went to bed, and said nothing to anyone.

7

ELDER'S SNACK BAR

I could see Dad look up when I got out of the cab. He watched the driver help me with my luggage. The sign, "Elder's Snack Bar," looked freshly painted. When we were little and driving around in the car, Dad would point out faded signs and burnt-out neon lights.

"Some people have no pride," he'd say.

One after another, the family—Mom, me, then Kirk after he got out of the service—all quit working at the diner. Kirk came home from the Navy a different man. Before he went in, Kirk had worked with Dad, and like everybody else, stopped because of Dad's treatment. When he got out of the Navy, I was surprised that he went back to the restaurant. This was years after I had stopped working there. They struck a deal in which Dad would gradually relinquish control, and Kirk could run it as he saw fit. And Kirk had lots of ideas to improve sales.

It was during the summer, and I was home from college until the fall. Kirk and Dad had a furious argument over something about the restaurant. I never knew exactly what, but I'm sure Dad either resisted Kirk's suggestions or was not turning authority over to Kirk on the timetable Kirk felt that they had agreed to. Kirk never talked about it.

They were in Dad's bedroom. Kirk was screaming so loudly the neighbors on both sides of the house came to their windows.

"I'll never work for a piece of shit like you again!"

No one had ever yelled at Dad. Not ever. And no one sure as hell had ever called Dad a "piece of shit." Someone, I said to myself, would die tonight. But I didn't hear any response from Dad.

"I said, you are a piece of shit!"

Still no response.

"A worthless piece of shit."

Silence.

"Nobody in this house wants to work for a worthless piece of shit like you."

More silence.

"You make promises and now you're fucking going back on them. You're nothing but a Goddamn lying worthless piece of shit."

Still, I heard nothing from Dad.

Kirk screamed and ranted for what seemed like forever. If Dad said anything back, it was too faint to hear. Kirk fired 'F' bombs. He called Dad a bastard, a son-of-a-bitch, said he hated him and that "everybody else does, too."

Kirk stomped out of the room. It was the last time he worked at the café and the last time Dad and Kirk had said anything to each other.

Dad was standing at the grill when I walked in. It was now just after rush hour, with three or four customers sitting around the counter.

"Hi, Dad."

The customers looked up.

"Hey, Randy, I didn't know you had a son." I introduced myself and shook their hands.

"What are you doin' here?" Dad said.

"I came to talk to you," I said firmly.

"Okay." He looked surprised. Was he nervous, too?

"You want to put your luggage in the back?" he asked.

"No, I'm good. I'll just set it down here." I wouldn't be staying long.

He was wearing the same outfit—pants with small black and white checkers, white short-sleeve shirt, white apron, and paper diner hat—that he wore every day for over fifteen years. His hair was still thick, but now completely white. He stood erect and strong as ever—still in charge. The place was neat and organized, everything in its proper place—the result of the accumulated wisdom of decades of trial and error and constant improvement.

"You're either gettin' better," he'd say, "or you're gettin' worse."

No, it's better for the coffeemaker to sit here rather than in arm's reach of the customers—a guy once tried to help himself to a refill and dropped the coffee pot, sending glass and coffee flying everywhere. No, the fly swatter should be down here—out of view—because "people don't like lookin' at fly swatters while they eat." And no, the smaller plates should be stacked and on the near side of the larger ones to cut down on the frequency of long stretches, saving a fraction of a second off meal prep.

He had a million tricks, hints, and shortcuts.

Put a little vinegar in the water when washing the windows, it helps prevent streaking.

Put a little water in the catsup bottles, not to cheapen the flavor or to save money. Heinz catsup is too thick and becomes messy. If it's not thinned out a little, customers have to work too hard to get it out of our rubber containers and after a lot of coaxing, it comes out in a burst, spilling way too much on the hamburger. The customer ends up just scraping if off. And that's wasted money.

Use wrapped butter packages. People will be less likely to waste the butter, and if you put a block of butter on a tray, people will cut it using their breakfast knife. Leaves crumbs in the butter, and looks unsanitary.

When you peel a boiled egg, make sure it's still warm and roll it around on the counter, but not so hard that you smash it. Just roll it around so that the shell is crunched all over. Then the eggshell will peel off as if you were peeling an orange.

Never let anyone in after closing time. He'll think he has special privileges and will start coming later and later. Others will see your closing times as a soft time, and you'll end up staying open an extra ten minutes.

And, within a few percentage points, he could predict, from the moment a customer walked in, the size of tip that would be left.

"Get out of here," I said, when he made that boast.

But sure enough, it worked with customer after customer.

"All right," I said, "that works fine with repeat business. You already know."

But he did it with amazing accuracy with people who had never before walked into the building. I asked him to explain.

"Men tip more than women. White people tip more than black people. Black men tip more than Spanish-speakin' women, and more than Spanish-speakin' men—but only just a little. Black men tip more than black women. Older people tip more than younger ones."

There were some other variables.

"Fat people tip more than thin ones." He didn't know why, but thought that they were happier.

And really old people were likely on a fixed income, and tipped carefully. There was a critical non-variable: service. Everybody, regardless of the expected tip, got good service. They were helped right away, their water re-filled without asking, and their coffee topped off. In other restaurants, the tip might vary according to service. But at Elder's Snack Bar, everyone was treated the same—with prompt attention and respect.

In walked a middle-aged Latina. "Ten percent," he whispered. And she did.

A heavy, young to middle-aged white man? "Fifteen percent." Bingo.

Young black woman. "Twenty-five cents."

"Twenty-five cents?"

"Young, black woman—flat rate. Doesn't matter what she orders or how much it costs. Twenty-five cents."

When she left, I lifted up her plate—two dimes, one nickel!

Years later, I read an academic study comparing the tipping habits of blacks and whites. It confirmed that, on average, blacks tipped less than whites, regardless of service quality, even if the server was black. Damned if an Ivy League professor hadn't vindicated the S.O.B. high-school dropout.

Outside, the restaurant looked exactly as it did when he first built it—still an aluminum shoebox. Only now it was painted a beige color. The building was supposed to last just ten years. But Dad kept climbing on top of the roof and, using tar, patched the leaks himself and kept extending the life of the structure by six years and counting. A few years after he built the restaurant, he bought the little house next door, and announced grand plans to expand "the family business."

"Someday we're goin' to double the capacity," he said.

It never happened. So Dad rented out the little house, eventually stopped talking about expansion, and no longer called it "the family business."

It didn't start out as a restaurant. When we moved out of our first house, Dad kept it and rented it out. He lost count of the times he had Mom type out letters demanding late rent payment.

"What makes a son-of-a-bitch think he can live somewhere for free?" he'd say.

Dad and Mom discussed other options, including selling it, to "get it out of our hair." Then Dad discovered the area was zoned for "light industry." He started talking about knocking down the house and putting up a restaurant.

Mom fought it hard. "You must be crazy. Who builds a restaurant in a residential neighborhood?"

"If you have good food, people will find you."

"The busy street is Pico. Randolph, that's two blocks away! You can't see the restaurant from there."

"People have to eat."

"They have to find you first."

Down came the house. Up went the restaurant.

That was that. His proud little oasis was flanked by houses and a couple of apartment buildings. There was a small shirt factory a couple of doors down. But that was it as far as other businesses within several blocks. To the loyal and appreciative customers, it was a hungry man's Wrigley Field.

When we lived here, the area was maybe 40 percent black, 40 percent Hispanic, and the rest white. The combination of blacks moving out and lots of legal and illegal Hispanics moving in, made the area—near what is now the Convention Center— almost completely Hispanic, gang infested, and much more dangerous. A few years before Dad retired, he began getting up a half hour earlier to paint over the graffiti that cropped up almost every night. It became a battle of wills, the gang "graffiti artists" versus my Dad. But when the bangers saw that this old man would, like clockwork, erase their artwork the very next morning, they finally stopped. Dad won.

The café was a robber's dream, squeezed into a residential area surrounded by houses and apartment buildings. The traffic was light. But Dad was never the victim of a walk-in stick-up and was never mugged going in or out of the place. Late at night, the café was broken into and triggered the alarm over a dozen times in thirty-five years. But no one ever walked in with a gun.

At night after closing up, he walked out with the day's receipts—cash and coins—in a heavy bag. He used a shopping bag so, he said, it wouldn't be so obvious that he was carrying money. But everybody knew. Neighborhood tough guys and gang bangers often loitered in the small parking lot attached to the café. But no one ever threatened or approached him. When they were little kids, Dad handed them free vanilla ice cream cones out the back door. When their parents said, "Randy, I'm a little short today," Dad fed them on credit. They usually paid, but not always and rarely when they said they would. My mother used to get on Dad for "being taken advantage of." But they remembered.

"Hey, Randy. Let me get that for you."

Dad handed one of them his money bag. He held it, waited while Dad popped open the trunk, and handed back the bag.

"Thank you."

"No problem, Randy. See you tomorrow."

8

THAT FRIDAY

Dad looked at the clock on the wall behind the coffee warmers. "We close in about an hour. Sit tight. Somethin' to eat?"

"No, thank you."

"Still don't drink coffee?"

I shook my head. I was surprised he remembered.

"How about some tea?"

"Fine." I took out a newspaper and pretended to read it. And waited.

Francine brought the tea. She was a long-time waitress. I barely knew her and she always seemed uncomfortable around me—polite but awkward. This time was no different. I assumed over the years Dad had told her a bunch of shitty things about me and that she saw me through his eyes. When I worked there, she had just begun working part-time. I didn't think she'd make it. She was shy and way too fragile for my father. But she became his longest-running and most loyal and dependable employee. She lived around the corner. Her parents came here illegally from Mexico and spoke little English. Francine was maybe eight or nine when Dad opened the place. One day she walked in and scrambled up on one of the stools.

"Hi, Randy. My name is Francine. Someday I'm going to work for you."

She taught him enough Spanish so that my father could take anyone's order, no matter how complicated. The percentage of non-English speaking customers increased and Francine was on a first-name basis with everyone. She'd ask about their jobs, their spouses, and their children. She found part-time workers. My dad called her his "director of personnel."

Francine became full-time. During this time, I graduated from high school, went off to college and law school, settled in Cleveland, and never once called the restaurant. Francine knew because she answered the phone. How much, if anything, Dad told Francine about me, I didn't know. But she sure adored him. And I couldn't understand how anyone who worked with him could feel that way.

I thought about That Friday one last time.

Why that day, I can't say. He had cursed at me in front of customers plenty of times, as he had the day before and the day before that. But that day, That Friday, I just decided I'd had enough. But I'd had enough many times.

This time I was going to curse back, I always promised myself. Then he'd curse, and I'd just go in the back, slam something down, come right back out, and take some more.

"I'm not taking any more of his bullshit," I'd tell myself. But three or four "Goddammits" later, I hadn't said a word.

But that day, That Friday, would be different. It was rush hour, and the place was packed—a customer on every stool and another customer standing behind each one seated, waiting to order "to go."

Rush hour was like a tranquil day that turns into wind and

hail. You knew it was coming. But some days it started at 11:30. Other days at 11:30, the place looked deserted. Sometimes, everybody seemed to come in at 11:40. I remember a rush hour starting as late as 12:05. But you knew it was coming, and you'd brace yourself to wait on twenty hungry people with forty-five minutes to order, eat, and get back to their jobs. I felt guilty when I caught myself looking at the clock and wondering "when"—even hoping that today will be the day when nobody comes in. No rush hour today. Just once.

"I'm not runnin' a Goddamn charity," Dad would say. "Rush hour makes money. No rush hour and it's back to moppin' floors and cleanin' toilets. Do you want that?"

That Friday was hot. I never saw a day that busy. Rush hour began a good twenty minutes early.

The hot dog buns started it.

When he prepared a hot dog or chili dog, he'd lean forward, reach slightly above his head, grab a bun with his left hand, and stick his thumb in the opening just enough to slide in the wiener with his right hand. This time he reached, and found an empty box.

"Hot dog buns!" he called out.

Minutes earlier, he had asked me to refill the dwindling stack of buns, but I was taking orders and the phone was ringing. Run out of buns, and his rhythm is shot. And, as usual, buns were his fourth or fifth instruction—with at least two or three given when I was in the back and could barely hear. He rarely looked up when issuing a command, especially during rush hour.

"Did you say something?" I asked, coming in from the back where I went to get eggs.

"Brew another pot of coffee."

"Answer the phone."

"Bring me a bag of fries."

"Put up a container of ice cream."

"And where, Goddammit, are the hot dog buns?"

He spat out the orders like the drill instructor in *Full Metal Jacket*, only Dad was more intimidating. Lord help me if I got the orders in the wrong order. But what's the correct order? Hot dog buns must be dealt with first. I think.

"Fresh coffee pot!"

"I need the ice cream!"

"How many times do I have to ask for the Goddamn hot dog buns?!"

Prioritize. Read his mind. Don't make him ask twice.

"Where are the buns?!" he asked for the fourth time.

I finished taking the phone order, placed it on the order wheel to the left of the grill, quickly walked toward the back, and grabbed four cartons of buns.

"Where are the buns!?" Five times.

He had left the water running where we wash the dishes, and the sink had just begun to overflow. I put down the buns. I shut off the water, unplugged the sink to let some of the water drain, grabbed a mop, and quickly wiped the area dry. More than even roaches, ants, and potato bugs, he hated anything on the floor—grease, milk, water—that could cause a fall.

"Goddammit, I . . . said . . . bring . . . me . . . some . . . buns!"

I put down the mop, turned around, and started to pick up the buns—then I stopped. I untied the strings around my waist, took off my apron, and removed my paper hat. Full house, rush hour, phone ringing, and my father alone—I walked out.

"Now let's see how what happens," I said to myself. Sitting at the bus stop, I felt weak and stupid and cowardly. Why hadn't I said something? Anything? What a fucking wimp. What would happen that night when Dad got home, I had no idea.

"Go back," Mom said when I got home.

"Go back?"

I told her what happened. I thought she'd agree with me and support my decision.

"Go back," she insisted.

"What!? How can you tell me to go back when you couldn't take it?"

She said that there was a difference between the way a man treats his wife, and how he treats his son.

"No there isn't," I said. "They both should be treated like human beings."

I quoted her many condemnations of Dad, using her own words from when she'd worked there.

"And now you're telling me to go back?"

"Please," she said. "Your father needs you."

"No. He doesn't need anybody."

That night, I lay on the bed, trying to read, waiting for him to come home. I thought about not being there when he got home. But I was already angry for not confronting him then and there, and walking out like a little coward. No, I'll be here when the son-of-a-bitch gets home. I'm not running.

I looked up and he was standing at the door—big, tall, and angry. He could have been there for two seconds or it could have been minutes. He didn't come in.

"Why . . . did . . . you . . . leave?!"

"I got tired of being cursed at. I got tired of being treated like an animal. And I'm not going back until you start treating me like a human being." I had never talked to him like that.

He was furious. He reached into his wallet and pulled out a ten-dollar bill. Then he crushed it into a ball and threw it on the bed. I didn't move to pick it up. We just stared at each other. I picked up my book.

"You're on your own," he said.

He turned and walked away.

"Okay," I said to myself as he left my bedroom That Friday. "I'll manage without you. You're not going to stop me, you son-of-a-bitch. I'm stronger than you think. I'll show you."

I made another promise. I was never going to be like him. Never.

That was the last time we spoke to each other—for ten years.

I looked at the clock and folded the newspaper that I had pretended to read. Francine said good-bye and left for the day. Dad turned off the grill and the fryer and the oven. He unplugged the toaster and poured a cup of coffee. He went out of the back door and came in the front, locked both doors, waved away a tardy customer who was approaching, and flipped over the "Open" sign in the window. He sat down on the stool next to me.

It was 2:30.

· PART TWO ·

THE TALK

9

THE BEGINNIN'

"What kind of father do you think you are?" I asked. I didn't feel nervous. That surprised me. What I felt was anger.

"Is that what you came out to ask me?"

"That's what I came out to ask you."

"What kind of father do you *think* I am?" he said.

"Compared to what?"

He laughed that laugh. The real one that came from down home. It had been a long time since I'd heard it. I sure didn't expect that.

"You know that we were all afraid of you," I said.

He stopped laughing and put down the coffee.

"What do you mean?" he said after a long pause.

"I mean, we were afraid of you."

"Kirk and Dennis, too?"

"Scared to death."

He shook his head. He didn't know?

"C'mon Dad, it's hard to believe that you don't know this."

Another long pause. He stirred his coffee even though it was black. Was he nervous? Good. How does it feel?

"That's it? That's why you came all the way out here? To tell me that?"

"No, that's not it. I—"

"Wait a second. Let me say somethin'. Then you can finish."

"All right."

"Look, I was tough. Not goin' to deny that. But, no, I didn't know you were afraid of me. All three of you?"

"All three of us."

He shook his head again. "Well, I'll say."

"You don't think we had any reason to be?"

"No, I don't. What did I do to make you afraid?"

What did I do to make you afraid? Was he kidding?

I let it rip. I told him about The Belt, the time I ditched it in the sewer. I told him about the time Kirk and I ran away, the whipping with the telephone cord when Dennis and I were naked and wet. It poured out, words like "cruel," "severe," "abusive." I went from incident to incident, growing angrier and angrier, completely forgetting that I promised not to get emotional. He sat. He listened. Sometimes he shook his head.

"Why did you even have children? I mean, what was the fucking point?"

I'd never cursed at him. He stared at his coffee and said nothing.

After all my practice and prep, all the if-he-says-this-I'll-say-that, I didn't expect nothing. But that's what I got. So I kept going.

"What did you do to make me afraid?" I repeated his words. "What did you do to make me afraid?" "What didn't you do to make me afraid?"

Your temper, Dad. The trauma of going to the drive-in. The scary curb feelers.

"I don't remember that," he said, after I told him about the time we wailed when he pretended that he was going to whip us.

"You don't remember that?"

"No, I don't."

"I didn't make it up."

No, after a million mental rehearsals where I told the son-of-a-bitch off, after all the times I imagined this moment, I didn't expect silence. I thought he'd deny, defend, blame Mom, maybe yell, or stomp off. But he sat there, absorbing story after story, remembering some things, but not most of them.

"I'm goin' to get another cup," he said, finally getting up from his stool. "You sure you don't want anythin'?"

"I'm good, thanks."

He went around to the back, poured another cup, set it on the counter, and came back around the front.

"How much time do you have?" he said.

"As much as you need."

He looked at the clock. "I guess I can put off cleanin' up for a while."

He took off his glasses and rubbed his eyes. He inhaled a couple of times. "You sure you want to hear this?"

"Go ahead."

Nothing he could say would change what he did or how he treated us. I came here to tell him what he did, and what a poor excuse of a father he was. He can say what he wants. Excuses won't matter. It's too late. Maybe this whole thing was a waste of time. Closure—what a stupid fucking concept.

"You know," he said, "I was afraid of my father."

He never talked about his father. When I was little, I used to wonder if his father was afraid of him, too.

"I promised myself when I had kids," he said, "I was not goin' to treat them like my daddy did me."

It was beyond strange to hear him say, "daddy."

"And do you think you treated us better than your father did?"

"I know I did."

That's delusional, I said to myself. Absolutely delusional.

"Why don't I start at the beginnin'," he said.

He was born in Athens, Georgia. That much I knew. And I knew that he was an only child. Beyond that, neither he nor my mother talked about his childhood. Whenever I asked, I got a one- or two-word response. The topic was off-limits, and after a while I stopped caring. Besides, what difference did it make? Whatever his background, whatever he went through, why exact vengeance on us? Whatever happened in his life, we were innocent bystanders. We were blameless.

"You were afraid of your father?" I said.

"I thought I told you all this before."

He hadn't. I knew next to nothing about him.

"Elder isn't really my name. I don't know what my real last name is. And if you didn't have a daddy, kids called you, behind your back, an 'outside kid.' So it hurt, hurt a lot."

Elder, Will Elder, was one of the many men his mother "took up with."

"You never saw your biological father?"

"No. And whoever he was, he didn't leave us. He was never around to leave. I never knew him. Never saw him. Least not that I can remember. And when I asked my mother about him, she changed the subject. So I just gave up askin'."

"Why use Will Elder's name out of all of them?"

"He was in my life the longest. So I just started usin' his last name, I guess."

They lived briefly on a farm where Will worked as a sharecropper. Dad helped work in the field picking cotton during the summer and after school.

"But then we moved to town."

"Why?"

"Don't know. Rent, I think. We couldn't pay. We moved a lot, you know, one step ahead of the landlord. I was fine with leavin' the farm because I hated farmin'. Wanted nothin' to do with it."

Dad didn't remember how long they stayed in Athens, but it wasn't long. Then it was off to Tampa, Florida.

"Why Tampa?"

"Will Elder got a job workin' construction. I think they were buildin' a bridge or a highway or somethin'."

Dad kept referring to him as "Will Elder." Will Elder did this. Will Elder said that. Will Elder worked there.

"Did you call him 'Dad'?"

"I called him Daddy because my mother made me. But I knew he wasn't my father. In fact, for I long time, I didn't know who my mother was."

He spoke softly. A man tapped on the door and Dad pointed to the sign: "Closed."

"You didn't know who your mother was?"

"Or, let me put it this way, I thought the wrong person was my mother."

He was playing in the yard with some kids. He looked up and noticed his aunt coming down the street toward the house where he and his mother rented a room.

"Yonder come Aunt Covey," he shouted. The woman, his mother's younger sister, visited from time to time.

"That ain't none of yo' aunt," one of the kids said, "that's yo' momma."

"No it ain't. Nanna is my momma."

"That ain't what my momma said."

"Well yo' momma is a lie."

"No she ain't." Other kids joined in and sided with the kid. "No she ain't!"

"Yes she is."

"No, she ain't. Yo' momma is Covey. My momma said so, too."

"So did mine," said another.

"She's a lie, too."

"Don't you call my momma a lie."

"Well, she is too a lie."

This led to a fight. After the scuffle, he ran into the house.

"Nanna, they say you ain't my momma. Tell me they lyin'."

"Ran, sit down."

Nanna admitted that she was really his grandmother, and that Covey was not his aunt, but his mother. Everyone knew it, except my father.

"Why were you lied to?" I asked.

"It was a shame not bein' able to raise your own kid. And Covey, my mother, had me—as they say—illegitimately. That made it even worse. In those days, people wouldn't even let their kids go into the home of a woman who had an 'outside kid.' Covey didn't have the money to raise a kid and I didn't have a daddy. So I lived with Nanna. For some reason, it's less of a shame to be raised by a grandmother than a single mother."

"How old were you when you found out who your mother was?"

"Five."

He said nothing for several seconds. And then he pulled a paper napkin from the little dispenser on the counter.

"'Scuse me. Sorry about that."

It was the first time I'd ever seen him cry. I didn't know

he could. Here he was, wiping his eyes, almost unable to speak. What should I say? "It's okay, Dad?" "Are you all right, Dad?" What? I didn't say anything.

"When I found out," he said, "I couldn't stop cryin'."

He loved his grandmother. She made him feel loved and safe. He didn't even like Covey, who seemed to pop up from time to time, never staying long and never really showing any affection toward him.

"I think I'm from some man she barely knew. Doubt she even knew which man. If she did, I think she looked at me and maybe I reminded her of him."

One day, Covey came for him.

"I ran outside. They didn't find me for three hours."

He told Nanna that he didn't want to leave her. But Covey took him.

He stayed with her for a couple of weeks. She ran out of money and returned him. Then she came back, kept him for a couple of months, and returned him again. This went on for at least a couple of years. One day, she came for him for good. It was the last time he saw his grandmother. It was the last time he felt secure.

Again we sat, silent, for several seconds. He pulled out another napkin.

"What name did they write on your birth certificate?" I asked.

"What birth certificate?" He laughed, "I wasn't born in no hospital like you kids—with a doctor and nurses. People down there used a midwife. Nobody with any trainin', just somebody who seemed like she knew what she was doin'. I was born in a room we rented."

There is no record of his birth, not even a line written in the family Bible. There was no family Bible. Covey and Nanna were illiterate.

"How do you know your birth date?"

"I don't." He knew the year, but didn't know the month and day.

When he enrolled in school, the lady who registered him asked him his date of birth.

"'Don't know,' I told her. 'Okay,' she said, 'May 25.'"

"Why May 25?" I asked.

"It was that lady's birthday."

"Well, I guess she had a one in 365 chance of getting it right."

He laughed. "As long as I wasn't born on the last day in February in a leap year. With my luck, I probably was."

"What kind of father was Will?"

"Only half worked, drank and—well, he was a bad drunk."

"Abusive?"

When Will got his paycheck, he'd bring it home where Covey would keep it to prevent him from gambling it away. Then he'd get drunk and demand it back.

"Why she wouldn't give it to him, I have no idea. He'd beat her and take it. Then the next time he got paid, he'd bring her the check, get drunk, beat her, and take it back. She knew she'd get a beatin', but she never gave it back—least not right away. Damn silly."

"'Please give it to him,' I used to say. 'Please just give it to him.' She'd say, 'No, we got to eat.'"

This ritual re-played itself over and over. He brought home his money, gave it to Covey, got drunk, beat her, and took the money back, then gambled it away. Dad tried to intervene "a couple of times," but he was small and got knocked to the ground. Covey told him to "stay out of it."

"Did he beat you, too?"

He did.

"And it could be over the silliest thing, and he did it when he was drunk or sober. He beat me once for not callin' him 'sir.' It was 'Yes, sir' or 'No, sir,' or else get a beatin'."

"What did he beat you with?"

He balled up his hands. "His fists."

I shook my head.

"But I'll tell you, I promised myself when the time was right, I was goin' to kill him."

After Tampa, the work ended for Will Elder. So he put my dad and Covey in his old car. Through relatives, he had arranged a construction job in Memphis. But the car broke down several times along the way before konking out completely in Chattanooga. It would be days, if not weeks, before it could be repaired. And there was no money to fix it anyway. So the car just sat, and Will Elder found work. They rented a room and stayed in Chattanooga.

Then one day Will was gone. His mother cried for days, but soon another man moved in. Then he left and another moved in. One day, my dad came home from school.

"And I just resented the son-of-a-bitch bein' there. I took off one of my boots—plop!—dropped it loud on the floor. The man said, 'Stop all that noise.' I took off the other one—plop!—dropped it."

"Dammit, boy, stop makin' all that noise!" the man said.

"I will not. This is my room, not yours."

"He's right, boy," Dad's mother said, "stop makin' all that noise."

"This is my room. He should just leave."

"No, it ain't, it's my room. And I'll have who I want in it. Now quiet."

"Then I'm leavin'," my dad said.

"Hah, good. Take your hungry ass away from here," Covey said.

Dad got dressed, put a few things in a sack, and walked out.

As he walked down the street, Covey shouted at him through the window. "You'll be back! Else either be in the cemetery or the penitentiary."

Dad turned to me and raised his right hand. "And as my hand is to God, I've never spent a day in my life in jail. But I never went back. And I ain't dead—yet."

He was thirteen the day he left home.

10

A HARD-ASS LIFE

I remembered Dad sending his mother money. When I started working for him, every Friday he'd hand me an envelope with her name and her Athens, Georgia, address.

"Take this to the mailbox," he'd say.

"What's in it?" I once asked.

"Do as I say and just take it and put it in the mailbox."

So I asked my mother. "Your father sends his mother money every week. I don't know why, the way she treated him. And we could use that money."

But every Friday he handed me an envelope, and every Friday I'd put it in the mailbox.

I started to ask him why he did it, given the way she'd treated him, but I wanted to hear what happened after he left his mother. I had so many questions. You left home for good? What about school? How did you survive?

"Weren't you scared?"

"Didn't have time to be scared."

He had already decided to stop going to school. Through the eighth grade, all the boys wore short pants. When the school year started for the ninth grade, everybody wore the "long pants." But his mother couldn't afford them and resented him for wanting them.

"What's wrong with yo' shorts?" she said. "Ain't no holes in 'em."

He explained that it would be embarrassing to wear them. Nobody—no matter how poor, "and everybody was poor"—still wore shorts in the ninth grade.

"Only thing that's embarrassin' is you," she said. "I ain't buyin' no long pants. You get you a job and buy yo' own damn pants."

"Wouldn't you have to drop out of school to get the money for the pants?" I asked.

"She didn't care. I already had more 'book learnin' than she did, and she thought school was a waste of time."

"What happened to your mother?"

He said at some point, Covey went back to Athens, where she had friends or family. There, Covey had someone write a letter to give Dad her address. "Outside of the time I went to see her when I got out of the service, I never saw her again."

"Oh." I wasn't sure what to say.

"Anyways, when I left, that's when I went up on the mountain and started lookin' for work."

"The mountain?"

The mountain, he explained, was Lookout Mountain in Chattanooga, "where some white families with a little bit of money might give me some work."

The thirteen-year-old knocked on doors, did odd jobs, and slept in barns—anything to make a little money.

"I'd eat shit with a splinter rather than to go back to that room with my mother and the boyfriend."

Soon a family hired him full-time to clean around the yard,

hoe the garden, and pick berries. The family also had a cook and she made more money. Plus she worked and slept inside the house, which was a lot more comfortable than his place on the floor in the barn. After chores, he'd sit with her in the kitchen, watch her prepare dinner and bake desserts, and ask questions. When nobody was home, he'd go in the kitchen and try to prepare a meal.

"At first, everythin' came out bad. I'd throw it away and start again. Fix somethin', throw it away. I don't know how many cakes and pies I ruined. One day, the cook got sick and left the house for several days. So I made dinner—meat, sweet potatoes, greens, and baked a cake. The man of the house sat down at the table. After dinner, he said, 'I guess she's feelin' better now. That girl really outdid herself this time.' The woman said, 'That wasn't none of her' and she pointed to me, 'that little rascal fixed all this.' 'Well,' the man said, 'we got ourselves a new cook.'"

He never did yard work again. He became popular with the family's friends who came for dinner. He improved and learned fancier dishes. He asked for more money. The family refused. He left and started working for another family at twice the money.

"After a while, I wanted more money. So I decided to leave the mountain for town, to see what I could pick up."

He worked a bunch of jobs, each one paying more than the last. First he shined shoes. "I knew I could do better, so then I started deliverin' ice."

A "cheatin' black man" hired him to drive a horse-drawn delivery cart to carry blocks of ice, which people used to put inside their home "ice box"—a big container where food was placed below and around a block of ice.

"It got so the guy half wouldn't pay me. I was drivin' those horses all day and half the night. And he still half paid me and never on time."

After weeks of no payment or partial payment, the boss owed my father $3.10. "You don't know. $3.10 durin' the Depression. Shi-i-i-it."

He kept asking and kept getting put off. The man operated out of a little office, and Dad went there "to see about my money." While the secretary "or assistant or whatever she was" made Dad wait, the man sneaked out of a back door. It was a maneuver, Dad later learned, that the man and the secretary pulled many times on other employees. Most workers just quit and wrote it off as a lesson learned. The man just hired someone new and repeated the process.

"I said, 'Shi-i-i-it, I'll be damned.' I went and got me this piece-of-crap gun—probably would have blown up in my face if I'd 'a shot it—and this time I went though his back door. He was sitting at his desk.

"'I want my money,' I said.

"'I don't have it,' he said.

"I said, 'I want my Goddamn money!'

"He started to get up, but I pushed him back down. I pulled up my shirt to show him the gun."

Shaking, the man reached in his drawer and counted out three dollars.

"Then I said, 'And I want my damn dime!'"

A man with two little boys walked by on the sidewalk, saw my dad and I, and waved.

"Don't know the father's name," Dad said, "but the kids are Carlos and, I think, Juan. On hot days, I give them ice cream cones."

The kids were bouncing up and down, "Hi, Randy!"

After the ice delivery job, he worked as a bowling pin "set-up man." Before the days when machines picked up and re-set the bowling pins, a guy at the other end of the lane rolled the ball back and manually set up the pins.

"Whites only?"

"There was a black bowlin' alley, but you couldn't make this kind of money. Anyway, did that for a few months."

The bowling alley was directly across the street from a hotel.

"I used to watch the valets run to the cars, get out the bags, and collect tip money from the folks checkin' into the hotel. 'That's for me,' I said to myself. There was a black hotel, but you couldn't get this kind of tip money."

He got hired.

"Pretty soon I was doin' everythin'. I took bags up to the rooms, made the beds, cleaned the rooms, swept the floors, washed windows, pretty much ran the kitchen. Everythin' but check people in and out and handle money. Didn't trust 'you people' to handle money. But it got so that hotel couldn't run without me."

He did this for about three years.

"I worked every day, 365 days a year. Never took a day off. One day, Christmas Day, I didn't come in because I was sick as a dog. Guy wanted to fire me. I said to myself, 'Shit, one day off in three years and he wants to fire me. Hell, no.'"

He saw that some of the men left the hotel business and started "runnin' on the road." They became railroad Pullman porters. Pullman was the largest employer of blacks in the country. The company rejected far more applicants than they accepted. It was an elite job for blacks, and quite an honor to be hired as a Pullman porter.

"You had to be sharp."

They had a union, the Brotherhood of Sleeping Car Porters, led by A. Phillip Randolph. The first—and easily the most powerful—black union in the country, it pushed to improve working conditions for Pullman porters and for other working-class blacks.

"It was around that time I met your mother and—"

"Wait a sec," I said. "Didn't you room with Thurman first?

"Oh yeah. How did you know about that?"

"Thurman told me."

I got to know Thurman when I moved to Cleveland two years earlier to practice law. We became close friends. Until I lived in Cleveland, I had no idea that Thurman and my Dad once lived together.

My colorful Uncle Thurman is my mother's youngest brother and father of two daughters. Like my mother, he left the family's Huntsville, Alabama, farm and moved to Chattanooga. Thurman soon moved again, part of the largest voluntary migration of a racial or ethnic group of people in American history. Between the years just before World War I and after World War II until around 1970, some six million blacks moved from the agricultural south to the industrial north. One uncle moved to Detroit, another to Chicago, and another ended up in Washington, D.C.

Thurman also left Chattanooga to "go up north" to Cleveland. Within days, he found a job, one that lasted until his retirement almost thirty years later, with General Motors.

Until my life intersected with Thurman's when I moved to Cleveland after law school, I only had vague memories of him coming to L.A. once or twice to visit my mother. And I saw him a bit during the summers I spent on my grandparent's farm in Huntsville.

I learned that he not only met my father before my dad met and married his sister, but Thurman actually roomed with Dad for almost a year.

"You know your Uncle Eddie introduced them," Thurman said. "But I knew him before he met your mom. Me and your dad shared a room together. Eddie arranged it."

I'd never met anyone who knew my father, let alone someone

Dad knew before he met and married Mom. The stories were fascinating.

"What was he like?" I expected Thurman to say Dad was ill-tempered and difficult to get along with, and that living with him was a regrettable experience.

"He was the hardest-working, most straight-ahead man I ever knew. He didn't play."

Thurman said Dad worked like crazy, treated people fairly, and saved his money.

"How long did you live with him?"

"About a year. When you live with someone that long, you pretty much get to know him."

"And what did you think of him?"

"Your father would have five dollars when most mother-fuckers didn't have a dime. And he could dress! Pair of two-toned shoes, the best hats, had a pocket watch. He didn't go out that much, but when he did, man, dude was sharp. Never lied. Never pulled any shit. And he was funny! Could tell jokes without stopping for two hours.

"He had one of those fancy cigarette holders. He'd go into his pocket and take out a silver cigarette case. Pull out a cigarette and tap it against the case. You know, like they do in the movies. Then he put the cigarette in his holder. And slo-o-o-owly light the cigarette. Style! You know I mean?"

Once, when Dad was asleep, Thurman snuck in, went to the dresser and took the cigarette case and the holder.

"I wanted to impress a date."

He intended to return it before Dad awoke. On his way back to the room, Thurman patted his pockets. The holder was gone!

"Shit! I retraced my steps. Went back to the nightclub. Nothing. I knew he would be pissed. Had a right to be. It was expensive—had carving and shit all over it. I tried to find something that night like it—only cheaper—and sneak it back before he missed it. But nothing was open. Well, he was mad, but told me to pay him a little bit every week and we'd be square. I did, and it was never mentioned again. He was the most you-treat-me-right-I'll-treat-you-right-man I ever met."

He said Dad "loved children" and always wanted a family "because he never had one."

After I felt comfortable with Thurman, I told him that Dad gave me no money for college or law school, and that Mom complained about it.

"Wait a sec. Who paid the house note?"

"Dad." Mom, when she complained about "her bills," never said that she paid it.

"Who paid the car note?"

"Same thing. Dad paid for both their cars."

"Car insurance? Homeowner insurance? Utilities?" Dad, Dad, and Dad.

"All that food he brought from the restaurant?" Dad always brought home bulk cartons of things like milk, eggs, bacon, cereal, potatoes, and fruits and vegetables.

"Shit," Thurman said. "The reason your mother was able to give you money for school is that he was picking up the back end."

I unloaded, and told Thurman about Dad's treatment of my brothers and me, about my working for him at the restaurant, and about how he seemed cold and angry.

Thurman shook his head. "That's just his way. He had a hard-ass life. You ain't looking at this thing right. Least I don't think."

"SOMETHING MADE THE MAN CLOSE UP"

By now, so many people were going by outside, waving to Dad, and shouting out greetings that he suggested we go in the back for more privacy. I told him no, that I liked seeing how people felt about him. So we sat.

"You know, I lived with Thurman, too," I said.

"No, I didn't know that."

When I first moved to Cleveland, I stayed with Thurman and my Aunt Maggie for a couple of months while apartment hunting and familiarizing myself with the city.

"You never did tell me why you moved there," Dad said.

Why? Like all my moves—college three thousand miles away from home, law school in Michigan, choosing Cleveland after school—I wanted to be my own man, make my own mark away from you. I didn't want your input or your guidance. I didn't want you violating my personal space. Despite your treatment of me, strike that, because of your treatment, I was going to make it and make it big. So . . . fuck . . . you. If you want to know what I'm doing and where I'm doing it, ask Mom.

But I didn't say that.

"I don't know, Dad. It just seemed like a good opportunity."

"Well, you know what's best."

Jesus! All this time I'd waited to tell him how he screwed up, that he wasn't going to screw me up. But I just couldn't do it. I didn't want to hurt him. He'd been hurt enough.

"You know, a big Cleveland law firm made me an offer I just couldn't turn down."

"Well, you gotta go where the opportunity is. I always tried to. That's smart of you. Like I said, you know what's best."

The first day I stayed with Thurman the phone kept ringing.

"Shorty," my aunt's nickname for him, "phone for you."

An hour or so later, "Shorty, get the phone." Then again and again.

He'd pick up the phone and laugh, tell jokes, talk about work, and make plans. There were at least three more calls for him that evening, each time from a different guy.

"Thurman," I said, "you sure have a lot of friends."

"Not really. Just some dudes I know," Thurman said.

One "dude" lived down the street. They liked to work on cars together. Another guy was a former co-worker who left GM to start a carpet business. Another one, Bill, was a cousin. They had a love-nuisance relationship. When Bill left after visiting, Thurman would talk about how "slick" Bill tried to be, how he exaggerated his success and how he pretended to have more money than he had.

"But I like to play dumb around him," he said.

Thurman refused to be outsmarted. My father wouldn't have dreamed about keeping a friendship with someone like that. Dad would have called him "shifty" or "no-account." But Thurman enjoyed trying to outfox Bill and seemed to genuinely like him. Bill made Thurman laugh, but not in the way Bill intended.

I told Thurman that the only time my father ever received

a phone call was when someone broke into the café—and the alarm company called to tell him. When the phone rang, and my mother said, "Randolph, it's for you," it was bad news. Bet on it.

"Thurman," I said, "in one day, you've received more phone calls than my father has gotten since I've known him."

"That doesn't sound like the man I knew. Your Dad liked to have fun. He didn't like no fools around him, don't get me wrong. But something made the man close up."

"Thurman said that?" Dad said, as he waved to a couple of pretty scary-looking teenagers in leather vests.

"Yes. Was he wrong?"

He just shrugged his shoulders.

By now, Dad was on his third or fourth cup of coffee. I'd lost count. We had been talking for more than an hour. He smiled a lot, and spoke calmly. I no longer felt nervous.

An old lady came to the window and smiled.

"That's Elvia. First person to walk in here. Been comin' ever since."

She blew him a kiss. He laughed.

"You were saying how you met Mom."

"When I was cookin' up on the mountain—I came to town every two or three weeks to get a haircut. My barber was your Uncle Eddie. Eddie married your Aunt Juanita. Eddie introduced me to your mother, Juanita's little sister."

Long before he met Mom, Dad and Uncle Eddie had become good friends. They liked each other and enjoyed the other's company. Both were hard workers, driven, and ambitious. Eddie loved my father's wicked sense of humor—even though Eddie was often the butt of Dad's jokes.

Eddie was one of the first blacks in the area to get a telephone installed in his home. Dad called him and disguised his voice.

"Sir, this is the phone company."

"Yes, sir," Eddie said.

"We're testin' all the phones on your street, and I need you to say 'hello' into the phone."

"Hello."

"Uh-huh. Now I need you to set the phone down on a table and back away about six feet and say, 'Hello.'"

Eddie held the receiver an arm's length away. "Hello."

"Now sir," Dad said impatiently, "Please don't waste my time, I've got lots of phones to check today. Put the phone down! Walk about six feet away and say 'hello' three times as loud as you can. And I haven't got all day."

Eddie set the phone down and measured his distance. "Hello! Hello! Hell—"

Aunt Juanita walked in the room to see what the shouting was all about.

"What the devil are you doing?" she asked her husband.

Eddie pointed to the phone lying on the table. "The phone man told me to do it."

"Oh, shhh, that ain't nobody but Randolph making a fool out of you!"

Dad envied Eddie's marriage. Aunt Juanita "fussed over" Eddie and always kissed him when he walked in from work. She loved hearing him talk about politics and the stock market. They tried to have children, and then adopted a little girl.

"Whenever I walked in Eddie's home, everythin' looked so nice. And that little girl was so happy. That's what I wanted."

So Dad asked Eddie to introduce him to his wife's sister.

"I thought your Mom would be just like Eddie's wife."

"Dad," I said, "Mom's nothing like Aunt Nita."

"Now you tell me."

My mother attended a black college called Talladega in Talladega, Alabama. She spent one year there before running out of money. But one year of college might as well be a PhD for a southern black woman.

"When you went away to college for a year and came back, you were educated as far as everybody was concerned," Thurman once said.

Aunt Juanita never finished high school. She was in awe of her husband.

"Your mother," Dad said, "married 'down.' She never said that, but I know that's how she felt. You know what it's like to have your wife think that she should've done better?"

No, I said to myself, I don't.

"But there must have been a connection. Or you wouldn't have married her and she wouldn't have married you."

He just stirred the black coffee.

"What did you do on your first date?"

"I don't remember."

"Where did you go?"

"Don't remember."

"What did you think of her when you first went out? That she was attractive? That she was smart? You had to have a reaction."

"Well, I guess I thought she was pretty and all that, but I really can't say what I thought about her."

"Well, that's romantic."

He laughed. We both laughed.

"Not exactly Romeo and Juliet," he said.

"No, not exactly."

"Well, Romeo and Juliet didn't work out so well."

At first, he said, Mom enjoyed his sense of humor. But over time, she stopped laughing and started "just doin' like this." He rolled his eyes. "She was just puttin' up with me."

He paused. "You know, I'm not goin' to go into some stuff. You don't need to know all this."

He said I have a good impression of my mother and a "wonderful relationship" with her, and, "I'll be damned if I try to change it."

He stopped, stirred his coffee for a while, then continued.

"Right after we got married, I asked her if she loved me. She said, 'The only man I'll ever love is my father.' You know what it's like to hear somethin' like that?"

No, I didn't.

I suddenly flashed back to riding in the car with the family. The radio was on and Dennis was singing along. We drove under an overpass. This blocked the radio reception and caused the sound to completely fade. So for a few seconds, a horribly off-key Dennis serenaded us, a cappella.

"I used to wish I could sing," Dad said. "Now I wish you could."

Kirk and I laughed. Mom rolled her eyes.

I had forgotten about his humor. Between his eruptions, he was incredibly funny. Once he was holding a half-gallon carton of milk.

"Here, Larry, put this in the refrigerator."

He was looking away when I reached for the carton. But when my hand was six inches away, he released it. I scrambled like someone possessed to grab it before it hit the kitchen floor and splashed milk everywhere. I managed to catch it just before it crashed. The carton was empty. Dad roared. Mom rolled her eyes.

Another lady passed by the window and waved.

"Mrs. Ramirez," Dad said. "She lives in the apartment down the street. Has a son in the Army. Can't stop talkin' about him."

"Go home," she said. Dad nodded.

Eddie's shop, the Green Light Barbershop, also served as the unofficial neighborhood town hall for black Republicans. Uncle Eddie once told me, "No Negro in the South with a lick of sense was a Democrat."

"Is that why you became a Republican?" I asked Dad.

"No, I was a Republican before I met Eddie."

Dad was a Republican, and Mom a Democrat. It caused a lot of friction.

Dad would say, "Democrats treat you like you ain't got any sense. Don't nobody owe you a livin'." And, "It ain't right to give people somethin' for nothin'. I had less than nothin'. I know what that's like. You get up and keep pushin'. Don't nobody owe you a livin'. Democrats is ruinin' the country with all this damn welfare."

Mom would say, "You can't hold people back, and then say, 'I'm sorry, everything's okay,' when everybody else has gotten a head start." And, "The playing field isn't level. Some people have been crippled by the system and you can't say to them, 'That's just too damn bad.'"

Watching Mom and Dad talk politics was like watching like a tense tennis match—except when it was over, nobody shook hands or patted each other on the back.

Mom was a better and more informed debater. She read the *Los Angeles Times* and the *Herald Examiner* newspapers every day, and she subscribed to *Time* magazine. No one else in the neighborhood—that I knew of—subscribed to any newsweeklies. She'd quote Truman, discuss the Monroe Doctrine, and watch the quadrennial political conventions. I loved watching the conventions with her.

"Why do they wear hats and wave signs? What is a first ballot nominee? What is a delegate? Why do they always say, 'The great state of . . . casts its votes for . . .'?" She patiently answered my questions. She had her favorite anchors and reporters: Howard

K. Smith, Eric Sevareid, Chet Huntley, David Brinkley, and Walter Cronkite. We switched back and forth from one network to another, depending upon the anchor.

For kitchen table debates, my mother's one-year college education trumped the eighth-grade drop-out—at least in what my Dad dismissed as "book knowledge."

"That just don't make good sense," Dad would say when my mom argued for universal health care or what became known as affirmative action. "Democrats treat you like you ain't got any sense. They think you're too stupid to figure out how to get your own. Don't nobody owe you a livin'. Give people somethin' for nothin', you'll end up with nothin' for somethin'."

During the primary elections, the polling precinct set up separate voting booths for Republicans and for Democrats. Our polling place was the house across the street. It had at least ten Democrat booths to accommodate our near-100 percent neighborhood Democratic registration. It had but one lonely Republican booth that almost nobody used—except Dad. With everybody watching, he would request a Republican ballot and walk directly to the Republican booth and pull the curtains closed behind him. The place got quiet as the neighbors watched the deviant black Republican. He didn't give a damn. I saw that same little smile he wore when cooking at the grill.

Then came Watergate. It changed things in the house for the worse.

"I don't see why this break-in thing is goin' to cost the man his job," Dad said.

"What!? He lied about it, tried to cover it up, and got other people to lie."

"Lied about some idiots breakin' in somebody's office. What did they do there? Steal money?"

"They broke into the office of the chairman of the Democratic

Party."

"So what? What does he know that Nixon didn't already know? Nixon didn't send them in there."

"What about the tapes?"

"What about them?"

"They prove he was in on the cover-up."

"Tell you what they should do. John Dean and Ehrlichman and what's the other one—Haldeman? Anyway, before they send them to jail, they should get together and make some new tapes and just replace the old ones. Then go on about their business."

"Are you serious?" Mom said.

"Damn right, I'm serious. What did Nixon do that hurt the country? And he's losin' his job over this. I bet a whole lot of presidents did worse. He just got caught. Should've burned the damn tapes. Now, it's too late to burn 'em. So, if I was Nixon, I'd make some new tapes."

"For God's sake, Randolph!" She walked out of the room.

They never discussed politics again.

"Yes," Dad repeated as he toyed with his coffee cup. "Your mother isn't easy."

We didn't say anything for a while.

"You never attended any of my graduations," I finally said. "Not junior high, not high school, not college, not law school."

"What?"

I repeated it.

"Had to work. What, you don't think I was proud?"

I shrugged.

"I damn sure was."

He said that when I went away so far—the East Coast for college, the Midwest for law school—it became a matter of cost. He was right. How could I deliberately choose schools far away from home—to get away from him—and then get upset because of the cost to close up the café, lose money, and pay a for coast-to-coast flight to come visit?

I reminded him how he promised to try to make it to my junior high school graduation, but didn't. Mom came with Aunt Dorothy.

"When I got home I cried. I didn't think you gave a shit."

After high school, I never went to another graduation ceremony, just had the schools mail the diplomas.

"You went to just one Little League game."

"I remember, the one where you tore Kirk up."

It was so strange to see him in the stands that day. I heard him yelling all game long.

"Way to dig right in there!" he shouted. I used to be afraid of the ball, and it took me almost a half a season to overcome the fear of getting struck by a pitch.

"I also went to one of your practice games," he said.

He did?

"And you stood this far off the plate." He stretched his arm out. "You used to be afraid of the ball. By the time you were up against your brother, you were diggin' right in there."

He went to a practice game?

"And who sponsored the team one year? Elder's Snack Bar. Café helped pay for your uniforms."

I remembered. But I thought that was Mom's doing. But the café was Dad's place, for Chrissakes.

"Would I have sponsored the team if I didn't give a shit?"

Another man walked up to the glass and tapped on it.

"That's Rodriguez," Dad said.

The guy pointed to his watch as if to say, "Isn't it time for you to go home?" Dad smiled and waved him off.

"Do you love Mom?"

The question caught him in mid-swallow. I expected him to

say, "No," or "At one time I did."

"Yes, I do."

I said nothing.

"You don't believe it?" he asked.

"No, I don't."

"Suit yourself." His way of saying, "You're entitled to your own opinion."

"You have a helluva way of showing it."

"Your mom isn't easy."

I didn't say anything.

"Have you ever asked her if she loves me?"

"No," I said.

'Why not?"

"I guess I didn't want to hear the answer. How do you think she feels?"

"I'm just not goin' to get into that. I made my bed, and I'm goin' to lie in it. That's all I'll say. When you have kids, you have to be there for them. And I wasn't about to get divorced again."

"Again?"

"You didn't know I was married before?"

"What?"

"Matter of fact, I was married twice before."

"What?!"

"You didn't know that?"

Was he kidding? No, I didn't friggin' know he'd been married before. Twice!

He first married when he was nineteen. He married a nineteen-year-old girl who didn't tell her parents.

"Soon as her parents found out, they made her go to court and have the marriage—what do you call it?"

"Annulled?"

"That's it. She was young, and they wanted her to marry

someone 'better.'"

"Did you love her?"

"I did. Her family moved away right after the, what do you call—"

"Annulment?"

"Right. The second time, I married a woman who cheated on me."

"I assume this didn't last long either?"

"Seven years."

"Seven years!"

All this before he married Mom?

"Besides," he said, "I wanted kids and she couldn't have any. So it worked out. Least I think it did."

I needed to use the restroom. Given all the coffee he had drunk, I thought he was probably fighting it, too.

"You know, I left you guys for awhile one time."

"What do you mean?"

"I mean your Mom and I—I just decided to leave you all. We decided to get divorced."

My bladder could wait.

"When? I don't remember that. I would have remembered that."

"Well, I did. I decided that I'd had enough and that you guys would be better off without me around."

He found an apartment, put down first and last month's rent, packed, and left.

"How long were you gone?"

"Three days. Couldn't sleep. Couldn't eat. I just wasn't goin' to do to you what they did to me—make you grow up without a father. It's just not the same when your daddy ain't around. So I came back home. And nothin' more was said about it."

Well, I'll say.

It was 4:05.

HIS LIFE AND TIMES

"Why did you go into the Marines?" I asked.

"Everybody who could either got drafted or joined. I joined."

"Why the Marines?"

"They always seemed to be where the action was. And I liked the uniforms."

"Did you like being a Marine?"

He said at twenty-eight, he was older than most of the others in boot camp at Montford Point, a black training facility attached to Fort Lejeune.

"I was probably more disciplined than the rest of the guys. I had been out on my own so long."

He was made a cook, then promoted to sergeant and put in charge of the mess hall. He traveled in the Pacific Theater, ending up stationed on Guam.

"I've been all over the world."

On Guam, they counted down the days to what everyone thought would be the invasion of Japan. Expected deaths, both sides, were conservatively estimated at one million.

"Then the bombs fell."

Hiroshima and Nagasaki forced Japan's surrender and ended the war. When I read about the A-bombs in grade school, I never thought about where my Dad was when they were deployed, or how it changed the course of his life—and my life. Like most people of his generation, he never talked about his service and how America helped save the world from tyranny. He didn't think he did anything heroic. He did his job, came home, and started up again.

"What did you think when you heard about Hiroshima?" I asked.

"I was confused. I didn't know what it meant. Pretty soon, we figured it out. It meant we were goin' home soon. And I could get married."

He and Mom wrote and made plans for marriage. In a shelf in the closet at our first home, I saw Dad's postcards from Guam that Mom kept in a photo album. When I asked her, she didn't want to talk about them.

"Put that old stuff away," she'd say.

The cards are long lost or thrown away. Mom probably didn't like thinking about how she may have felt something akin to passion for Dad—or maybe she didn't want us to think of her in that way. She was dismissive, even angry when I would ask her questions about those old postcards. So I stopped.

"I loved runnin' on the road," he said.

He smiled as he talked about the pre-war years he worked as a Pullman porter.

"I got to travel, see different parts of the country. It's why I moved to California."

"What was it you liked about California?"

"It was always so sunny. November. January. March. Didn't matter. Bright and shiny. And it seemed like the people were more fair. I didn't see any 'Blacks Only' signs. You could sit anywhere you wanted on the bus or in the movies. Looked like anybody could catch a cab. Plenty of work, night and day. So I made a mental note that maybe I'd move here."

Because he was single when he worked for Pullman, he agreed to "run wild." This meant he had no regular route or regular times, and it brought more hours and more money. He had to be ready at any time and be willing to go anywhere. He'd sometimes have a layover in a city for a half a day to a full day.

"If we pulled in to a southern city, I always made sure I had tin cans of food and some crackers 'cause you never knew whether you'd be able to walk into a store and buy somethin' to eat."

"Growin' up," he said, "segregation was all I knew. Where you went, where you ate, where you sat in a movie house, even the public parks. The black parks weren't as nice as the white ones—had more rocks and dirt."

Yet after the war, he returned to Chattanooga.

"I went to an unemployment office. When I got to the counter, the lady pointed to a sign I'd walked under. It said 'Whites Only.' 'You'll have to go through that door,' she said, pointin' to another one. So I walked back out the 'wrong' door and through the 'Colored Only' door. And the same white lady—the one who just told me I had walked through the wrong door—walked down to help me.

"I went home to your mother, and I said, 'Shi-i-i-it, I done traveled all over the world for this country, and I have to put up with this shit. I'm movin' to California.'"

He told Mom to stay in Chattanooga, and in four days he'd find a job and send for her.

"Why were you so sure you'd have a job in four days?"

"I know me."

When he got to L.A., he rode the streetcar and walked around for two days looking for work as a cook. Nobody would hire him. Every restaurant told him the same thing—he had no "references." He told them he ran the mess hall as a sergeant in the Marines. They all said, "Sorry, you have no references."

"So I changed tactics. Every restaurant I went to, I told them I'd work for a reference. They said, 'What?' I said, 'I'll work for a reference. If you like my work, you can start payin' me. Or, if you like my work but still can't use me, you can give me a reference.' They said, 'We can't let you work for free.' I said, 'I'm not workin' for free. I'm workin' for a reference.'"

"What happened?"

"Still wouldn't hire me. So, I changed tactics again. I didn't know the city very well and I was just catchin' the bus and walkin' around to get a job. That didn't make much sense. So, I went to an unemployment office. This time there was only one door, but the lady said she didn't have anythin'. I said, 'What time do you open?' She said, 'Eight o'clock.' I said, 'What time do you close?' She said, 'Five o'clock.' I said, 'I'll just sit right here until you close, and I'll be the first one here when you open. Just call me up here when you have somethin'.'

"I sat in the same chair for the rest of that day, and most of the next.

"Then she called me up. She said, 'I have something, but I don't know if you want it.' I said, 'What is it?' 'It's with the National Biscuit Company, but it's a job cleaning toilets.' I said, 'Of course I'll take it.'"

On his fourth day in L.A., he had a job. He sent for my mother.

He worked at National Biscuit for eleven years. It wasn't long before he was put in charge of the other janitors. He took a second full-time job as a janitor with the Barbara Ann Bread company. He eventually left Barbara Ann to work as a janitor for a business closer to home. The Paul Laymon Company repaired and distributed pinball and other coin-operated machines.

It had been years since I'd thought about Dad's job at Laymon's. It was just two blocks away from our first house, on the corner of Pico and Valencia. One Saturday, Dad asked Dennis and me if we'd like to go to work with him for a few hours. We didn't, of course, but what were we going to say?

Off to work with Dad we went. He opened the door to a large, dark warehouse. No one else was there. He turned on the lights. Everywhere we looked, there were pinball machines, just like the kind at Disneyland, all neatly lined up against the walls.

"These here haven't been fixed. But those over there, they work. Do you want to play them?"

Dennis jumped up and down so high, he almost ripped his Achilles. And I was looking for the catch.

"Dad, we don't have any change."

"Oh, that's all right," he said.

He reached in his pocket and pulled out a little tool, kind of like a bottle opener. He bent down, opened the front of the machine, inserted the tool, and jiggled something until he heard a "click." Cha-ching. The lights started blinking and the pinballs dropped, rolled down and lined up, ready for action.

"Let me know when you're done with that one, and I'll fire up some more."

Dennis and I went from machine to machine and spent the fastest four hours in recorded history. Dad disappeared to the other side of the building, but would re-emerge just in time to take out the tool and make another machine come to life.

Because his second job was two blocks away, he was able to get a little more sleep. He averaged four, sometimes four-and-a-half hours of sleep, six days a week. He also worked on most Sundays when he cooked, washed cars, or did yard work for Mr. Laymon.

"Your mother and I decided that she should be home with you kids—at least until junior high. So I had no choice. Didn't you like her bein' there when you got home from school?"

I did. And I'd known plenty of kids who came home to an empty house or to a relative or who stashed themselves somewhere until their mothers came to get them.

"When you don't sleep much, I guess it sort of makes you cranky. Least on Sundays—if you guys stayed quiet—I usually could get a little more."

This explains the Sundays we went tiptoeing around the house.

"Do . . . not . . . wake . . . up . . . your . . . father," Mom said.

I once had dinner with a wealthy, prominent California politician. He told me about his father who, like mine, left school and began working full-time at about fourteen years old. He got a job as a clerk in a department store. The store had a big inventory sale, and he worked thirty-six hours straight. The store manager, who found out about this enthusiastic hard worker, decided he was management material and took him under his wing. By the time he was in his twenties, he was the store manager. By his early thirties, he was put in charge of several stores and worked in senior management until his retirement.

My father, too, excelled wherever he worked. He'd propose different and better ways of doing things, which led to more responsibility. But then he'd reach a limit.

"Only so far 'you people' could go," he said. "The answer is to work for yourself. And that's what I intended to do. But I knew I needed more education."

So along with the two six-day-a-week jobs and his Sunday work, he went to night school for a high school equivalency diploma. I remember him sitting at the kitchen table "doing homework." I used to wonder—how could a grown-up have homework?

"I had a lot of catchin' up to do," he said. "I'd forgotten what little I knew."

Dad told me about how intimidating it was to go back to high school at his age.

"When I signed up for adult school, they asked me what grade I left off at. I said, 'I want to start at the bottom because I can't remember much of anythin'. So put me as low as you think you need to, and I'll work my way up.'" So they started him at the third grade.

Uncle Thurman, in Cleveland, talked about Dad's pursuit of his G.E.D. I told Dad how impressive Thurman had found it.

"You know the kind of balls it takes to go back to school when you're in your forties? I dropped out of high school," Thurman had told me, "and I always felt insecure about it. But I'll be damned if I'm going to work all day, do homework, drag my ass out of the house, and sit next to some teenager. Couldn't do it. Most motherfuckers wouldn't have the nerve. I know I didn't. But your father did."

"Thurman said that?" Dad said.

"He sure did."

"Well, I'll say. Huh. Never thought it was impressive. You just do what you have to do."

I asked about growing up in Athens, before he moved to Chattanooga. He remembered that it was a college town. And he remembered the University of Georgia.

"Did you ever go on campus?"

"No, it wasn't allowed."

"Did you ever think that maybe someday you could go to college?"

"No."

"Why not?"

"It's just not somethin' that ever crossed my mind, that I

could go to college, let alone that one."

"Does that bother you?"

"What, that I didn't think about college? No. I had to work. I did plan to be my own boss some day. That was my dream."

He noticed that black workers in Chattanooga walked long distances to and from their jobs. Why weren't their more jitneys to carry them back and forth? There were a few, but not nearly enough. He bought a used car but found out he needed a special license to operate a jitney service.

"You had to go to court to get it," he said. "So I filled out the application and went before the judge. He picked up my application and said, 'There's too many niggers out there tryin' to work. Denied.'"

It turned out that the judge was operating his own jitney service. He had hired black drivers to service black customers—and didn't want the competition.

"I didn't know this until later."

"What did you do after you found out?"

"What could I do? I just knew I had to figure out somethin' else. No point in givin' up over somethin' like this. That's what they want you to do—give up and just scuffle around complainin' about what the White Man did to me. Shi-i-i-it, I just had to keep on steppin' and figure somethin' else out."

He talked about the importance of financial independence.

"As long as you got money in your pocket and money in the bank, you're in control."

He used to hang out in bars and nightclubs with a couple of guys he thought of as friends.

"I'd pick up the tabs because I was the one who had money." One night they wanted to go out for another round of bar-hopping.

"But I told them not tonight, I was savin' to buy a car. 'Oh, that's all right, Ran,' they said, 'as long as you're with me, your money is no good.'"

So out he went. One friend paid for the first round of drinks, and then the second round.

"I'd gotten pretty drunk by then and they wanted to go to somebody's house where they were makin' bootleg whiskey."

The house was full of people laughing and drinking and dancing.

"C'mon, Ran, let's go upstairs," one of the friends said.

A bathtub upstairs was almost half full of homemade whiskey.

"Go ahead, drink up," his friend said.

Dad asked for a cup or a ladle or something to scoop up a drink.

"No, you don't need nothin.' Just lean over and drink all you want."

"The fumes were so strong I thought my head was gong to explode. I managed, I think, to take a gulp or two. But then I got dizzy and passed out."

He didn't remember how long he was out.

"When I woke up it was mornin'. Everythin' was gone—my coat, my watch, my wallet, my cigarette case, my holder, even the change I had in my pockets."

He walked to a restaurant whose owner he knew. She'd always been nice to him, eager to wait on him whenever he came in.

"I told her what happened and asked for money to get a ride home and for somethin' to eat. She said, 'I haven't made any money yet this morning. So there's nothing I can do right now.' I said, 'Okay, I'll just sit here until you make a couple of sales.' So I sat and one customer after another came in and ate, paid the bill, and left. After she rang up the cash register a bunch of times, I asked again. This time she said, 'Sorry, I don't give no credit.'"

He said he learned a powerful lesson.

"A dollar in your pocket is your best friend. I never forgot it, and I have never been on my ass since."

He reached into his back pocket, pulled out his wallet, and carefully unfolded a frail, yellowed piece of paper. He treated it like it was one of the Dead Sea Scrolls.

"Here." He put it in my hand. "Live by this, and you'll never be in trouble."

It was about three by five inches. How many times had he pulled it out and re-read it?

A. G. Gaston's *Ten Rules for Success*

1. Save a part of all you earn. Pay yourself first. Take it off the top and bank it. You'll be surprised how fast the money builds up. If you have two or three thousand dollars in the bank, sooner or later somebody will come along and show you how to double it. Money doesn't spoil. It keeps.

2. Establish a reputation at a bank or savings and loan association. Save at an established institution and borrow there. Stay away from loan sharks.

3. Take no chances with your money. Play the safe number, the good one. A man who can't afford to lose has no business gambling.

4. Never borrow anything that, if forced to it, you can't pay back.

5. Don't get bigheaded with the little fellows. That's where the money is. If you stick with the little fellows, give them your devotion, they'll make you big.

6. Don't have so much pride. Wear the same suit for a year or two. It doesn't make any difference what kind of suit the pocket is in if there is money in the pocket.

7. Find a need and fill it. Successful businesses are founded on the needs of the people. Once in business, keep good books. Also, hire the best people you can find.

8. Stay in your own class. Never run around with people you can't compete with.

9. Once you get money or a reputation for having money, people will give you money.

10. Once you reach a certain bracket, it is very difficult not to make more money.

I carefully refolded the piece of paper and handed it back to him.

"No, you keep it, and read it from time to time. It'll save you a lot of grief."

"Thanks, Dad."

"Need to go to the restroom?"

"You first," I said.

He got up, turned and stopped.

"Few more things: Hard work wins. You get out of life what you put in it. You can't always control the outcome, but you can control the effort. No matter how hard you work or how good you are, sometimes things will go wrong. Character is about how you react when they do.

"Now, if you don't mind, I'm goin' to the restroom."

· 13 ·

"YOU'RE A LOT LIKE ME"

Dad's story about the so-called friends and the bootleg whiskey reminded me of something I hadn't thought of in years.

"You were talking about the 'friends' who got you drunk and stole your money?"

"Yeah."

"I had a 'friend' like that."

I told him about Levi, a "friend" I had in the seventh grade. He was one of the cool students, very popular, and therefore had little time for a poot-butt like me. Nowadays, they call them "nerds."

One day Levi asked me for a dime. I gave it to him. The next day, he asked for another, and I gave it to him. Pretty soon, he started hanging around with me. The girls liked him, and every now and then one of them would actually notice me and say something to me. Mom bought me a beautiful long coat. We called them "car coats." They were not cheap, and most of the kids didn't have one. Levi asked if he could wear it. I let him.

"Pretty soon we were buddies. And this made me a little more popular."

"I bet that didn't last long." By now Dad, relaxed, had leaned back against the wall and propped his leg over another stool.

"One day, I said to myself, 'Am I that hard-up for companionship, that I actually have to pay for it? And what kind of friend takes advantage of another like that?' The next day he asked for the dime and the coat. I said, 'No.' And the kid started cursing me out. I just laughed at him."

"You know somethin'?" Dad said. "When people mistreat you, you put 'em down. You're a lot like me. Stubborn."

"You know, I used you to motivate me."

"Really?"

My high school, Crenshaw High, only taught a few, lower- and intermediate-level Spanish classes. A consortium of schools ran an experimental program called APEX—Area Program Enrichment Exchange—allowing students who had gone as far as they could go in a particular subject to go to other schools for advanced classes.

I had exhausted the Spanish curriculum offered at Crenshaw, and applied to spend a semester at Fairfax High for morning classes, one of which would be high-level Spanish. Fairfax, at the time, was almost completely Jewish and highly rated academically. Crenshaw was almost all black and did not share Fairfax's reputation.

"What did I have to do with that?" Dad asked.

My first day of Spanish classes at Fairfax, I was stunned at the level of competence. The teacher spoke only in Spanish, none of this half-in-English/half-in-Spanish like the teachers at Crenshaw. If you wanted to leave to go to the restroom, you asked in Spanish. If you explained to the teacher why your homework was incomplete, you did so in Spanish. So at my level, the kids were fluent. They didn't speak Spanish in the slow, halting stutter-step we did at Crenshaw. Fairfax demanded more from its students and, in turn, received more.

So I made, at best, mediocre grades on the tests leading up to the final, a book report on Don Quixote to be memorized and delivered orally—in Spanish, of course—in front of the class. Up to this point, I had fumbled and stumbled my way through, and the students felt sorry for me.

"By then, I was angry because I knew I was capable—and I realized that everything at Crenshaw was dumbed down. But my first day at Fairfax, I came home and told Mom and started crying."

"What did she say?"

"She said that maybe someday I could do something about getting these schools to raise their game. But in the meantime, I needed to get on the stick."

"She said the right thing," Dad said.

So I went to work on Don Quixote. I never spent more time on any homework assignment. I went over my grammar and made sure it was perfect. I rehearsed it in front of a mirror, and worked on my pronunciation.

"And I thought of you. I pretended you wanted me to fail. And I wasn't going to give you the satisfaction. The teacher was tough—like you. When you screwed up, she was brutal. So I imagined you standing up there at that desk with your arms folded when I walked up to give my report."

"I wanted you to fail? Why would I—"

I held up my hand. "Dad, I'm just telling you what I was thinking."

The day of the final, one kid after another stood up and delivered their oral report. After each speech, the teacher criticized.

"Mr. Rudin, you wrongly conjugated the verb, 'to be.'"

"Miss Hiller, you used future tense instead of the past tense."

Then it was my turn.

"Don't tell me," Dad said. "You went to town."

I did. The class got quiet. The contrast was night and day from the Crenshaw kid, who in his first week barely spoke, and the confident, poised young man standing before them. When I finished, the teacher said nothing. She just looked shocked.

"Well done, Mr. Elder," she said. "As for the rest of you, that's the way to do it."

In college, I suffered again because of my poor preparation compared to almost all of my classmates, who went to elite prep schools or quality public ones, like Fairfax.

"Imagine going to a school when everybody else went to schools as good or better than Fairfax—and they went to schools like that from kindergarten on."

Dad shook his head.

I was taking economics and statistics, two courses that required some background in basic calculus. The last math class I took was geometry in the tenth grade and when I decided to stop taking math, no teacher, counselor, or anyone else said anything about my decision being ill-advised. So at college, I took a calculus course at the same time I was taking economics and statistics.

"I would try to learn enough math at the same time I was learning the other two subjects."

On every math test, I scored a D or worse. My professor put a note in my mailbox to come see him.

"I suggest you drop out of the course," he told me, "before the semester goes past the time when you can quit without it going on your transcript."

I told him I needed it to understand the other classes I was taking.

"Well, the final counts for most of your grade, and you've done nothing to suggest you're capable of passing this course.

I'm meeting with you to protect you. I don't think you have it."

"What do I have to do on the final to pass the class?"

"You have to get a B. And I honestly don't see you doing it."

"Thank you for your concern," I said. "But I'm not dropping the class. I've never failed any course in my life, and this won't be the first. I intend to get a B on the final."

He sighed. "Up to you."

"What did you do?" Dad leaned forward.

"I wasn't going to be stopped, I told myself. Not by him, not by you."

A third-year math major named Marty lived upstairs in my dorm. We were friendly. I think we played ping-pong at the table in the basement a few times. He told me that he wanted to become a math professor at a "kick-ass" university. He aced every course he took, except one where he got a B. For "revenge," he took the advanced course in that subject the following semester, and redeemed himself with his customary A.

"I knocked on his door and told him what I told you, and asked if he would help me. We worked every night for the next couple of months."

"Why did he agree to do it?" Dad asked.

"I asked him that, too. He told me he knew he had a gift, but that his biggest gift was his work ethic. He said he felt obligated to help if he thought he could make a difference."

"Well, he was a teacher. Didn't you say he always wanted to teach?" Dad said. "That was his callin'. And he was usin' his gift."

Marty explained things so well, and in different ways. If one explanation made no sense to me, he'd suggest another way of attacking the same problem.

"You don't know how lucky you are to be able to go to school and learn—and to be around people like that," Dad said. "So, what happened?"

"What do you think?"

"Got a B."

"Yes, I did."

"Knew it," he said. "What ever happened to Marty?"

"I don't know."

"You should find out. Wouldn't hurt to thank him again."

"I will."

Next came law school.

The first year was intense. I decided I'd form a study group based on who impressed me most during the first few weeks of the first semester. One guy in particular stuck out. He was always prepared, volunteered answers, and, whenever a professor called on him, he hit it out of the park with his answers. I approached him after class.

"Jim, I'm forming a study group and I want you in it."

He looked down. "Well, I'm—I'm trying to assess, you know, assess my, my needs."

"He didn't want to waste his time with you 'cause he didn't think you had anythin' on the ball," Dad said.

"Right. And he probably wasn't wrong, but I was insulted."

We had something called Moot Court. Teams go against each other to make arguments before a group of actual appellate judges. It's pretty intense. You prepare and submit a brief, then present your case before the judges. The other team submits its brief and presents its case, and the judges lay into both sides' briefs and presentations. You've got to be quick on your feet, prepared to refute the other side's arguments and defend your own. My professor was preparing teams. I went up to him after class.

"Mr. Jim Hiller and I would like to go up against each other, if that's possible."

"I don't see why not. Okay, you can oppose him."

Jim never knew. I worked my tail off on the brief, tried to

anticipate every imaginable argument that Jim would make, and approached it like a boxing match. I pretended I was in training for the championship fight.

"Let me guess," Dad laughed. "You kicked the shit out of him."

"Damn right. I kicked his ass. He made an argument, I ripped it to shreds. He countered, I ripped his counter. I had him back-tracking and looking for the right cases to cite. He got hammered."

The judges complimented me on my brief and on the "quality and style of my presentation."

"'Mr. Hiller,' one judge said, 'you should have worked harder.' They ruled in my favor."

"What ever happened to Jim?"

"I told him later what I had done to make sure we were opposite each other. He was impressed. We became friends. We've stayed in touch. Sends me a Christmas card every year. He's with a law firm in Seattle."

"Well, I'll say."

It was getting dark outside. The bright indoor fluorescent lights reflected off the glass. I felt surrounded by mirrors.

It was 5:45.

14

"WOULD YOU DO THINGS DIFFERENT?"

"**W**ere you ever angry with Mom—the way you were with me?" he asked.

"Once," I said.

I stayed upset with Mom, for any length of time, just once—after she took Champ, our cocker spaniel, to the animal shelter.

He was our first dog. I was seven. We had just moved into our new house on Haas Avenue, and we now had a yard.

Dad brought home Champ in a cardboard box, a little black puppy with big brown eyes shyly staring up at his new family. Champ was quiet at first. But he broke out of that pretty quickly. We'd mock chase him, and he'd mock run away, cutting and ducking so we couldn't catch him. When we were exhausted and flung our tired young bodies down on the lawn, Champ would sit next to us, not even out of breath.

"Is that it? Is that all you got?" his expression said.

We loved coming home from school and having him run toward us and leap into our arms.

"He-e-e-re, Champ. He-e-e-re, Champ!"

But Champ had a problem.

When Mom hung sheets on the clothesline, Champ leapt up and nipped them to shreds. Mom swatted him.

"Bad dog! Bad dog!"

Champ would stop for a while. But soon Mom would find the new sheets torn into strips. Champ also jumped over the fence into our next-door-neighbor's yard, right into Mr. Lusk's onion patch, where the dog enthusiastically dug up the onions. Mr. Lusk sprinkled some brown powder with a noxious odor that was designed to keep dogs away. Not Champ. He smelled the stuff once or twice, developed a tolerance, and kept digging away at the onions.

"If that dog doesn't straighten up," Mom said, "I'm going to have to take him to the animal shelter."

We didn't take the threat seriously. But Mom complained about how much the sheets cost and that she "couldn't afford to run to the department store every week."

She tried shutting Champ in the garage, but he howled like he was being tortured. She tried chaining him to a tree, but he cried even louder. She tried indoors. Champ immediately planned his prison break.

"He-e-e-re, Champ!" I called one day when I came home from school. "He-e-e-re, Champ!"

Nothing.

"He-e-e-ere, Champ!"

"I had no choice," Mom said later.

I cried for three or four days.

"How could you?" we screamed.

We pleaded for Mom to go and get him back. She refused.

"Now, of course," I told Dad, "I know this decision wasn't made lightly, and would not have been made without you both agreeing."

"That's right," Dad said.

"But we were devastated."

"We didn't know what else to do. We didn't have the money."

The good news is that Champ led to Cream Puff. One Halloween night, a brown tabby kitten followed us from house to house as we trick-or-treated.

"Mom," I said when I got home, "this kitten followed us all the way home. Can I keep him?"

"Okay," she said. "What's his name?"

"Cream Puff," I said.

I couldn't believe it. She always said "no" when we brought home a stray animal and asked if we could keep it. Years later, she admitted that she felt horrible about Champ, so she promised herself that the next time we brought an animal home, no matter what—mouse, pigeon, or dinosaur—she was going to let us keep it.

Cream Puff was a beloved family member for almost fifteen years.

"And Cream Puff wasn't afraid of Mom. He'd bite her on the ankle if she was in the kitchen and didn't feed him."

Dad chuckled. "Maybe I should try that—bitin' her on the ankle."

We both laughed.

"Why have you never gone to church?" I'd wanted to ask him that all my life.

I never saw Dad set foot in a church. He never attended any Sunday services, though our church was only four blocks away. When we moved to Haas Avenue, he never even stuck his head in the door of our new church. My mother never asked him to go, at least not in front of us.

"When I was livin' in the country, my mother made me go

every week, sometimes more than once a week. The preacher was a big deal, the biggest deal there was. Wasn't no black doctor or lawyer down there, but if there was, he still would've been bigger. There wasn't nobody rich, no wealthy businessmen. The preacher was it! Strutted around like he was Roosevelt. All slicked up, smelled good. Wore nice suits, drove a fancy car, lived in the biggest house down there. This is durin' the Depression! How is it you end up rich bein' a preacher? Don't make no sense. It ain't supposed to be about money, supposed to be about people's souls. Right?"

"Right," I said.

"And he had all these women in the choir lookin' up at him and smilin' and shakin' their bodies at him when they was up there supposed to be singin'. And why do people wear their best clothes on Sunday, spend all that time gettin' dressed up, pickin' out what hat to wear? Who they supposed to be impressin'? God? It ain't no damn fashion show. They just showin' their neighbors what kind of clothes they have that you don't. What does God care about what you wear? Turned out the preacher was havin' affairs with two or three of them singers even though he was married and had a couple of kids. Damn near got shot."

I laughed.

"Most every week, I'd hear my mother gossipin' with her friends about who was sleepin' with who, and who had left his wife for who, and who she thought might be sleepin' with who."

He shook his head.

"They talked about that shit more than they talked about salvation. Damn soap opera. So I looked at all the crap that goes on—people like my mother givin' up their money that they work hard for all week—money that we needed. I didn't have no long pants to go to school, but she could give this man some money every week. People gettin' dressed up to show off, affairs goin' on with the preacher. And all the while the preacher standin' up there wavin' his arms and wavin' the Bible, supposed to be preachin' the Gospel. I said 'Shi-i-i-it.'"

"Not all churches have that kind of stuff going on," I said.

"More than you know."

"And even if they do, what does that have to do with you and your relationship with God?"

"It has a lot to do with it. If the man who supposed to be His messenger ain't followin' the message, how can he give it to me?"

"So you think people who go to church are fools?"

"To each his own. Count me out."

I asked him if he believed in God. I assumed he didn't, and that Mom reluctantly accepted, but didn't like, his lack of faith.

"Yes, I do," he said.

"Really?"

"Why does that surprise you? You don't have to go to church to believe in God and to try to do right by people. Some of the biggest sinners show up right on time on Sunday and walk in the church—and then go right on sinnin' when they walk out."

"Why did you send money to your mother every week," I finally asked, "after the way she treated you?"

"She's my mother, brought me into the world. She had problems. Just didn't know what she was doin'."

"Was it your way of saying, 'I made it—even though you kicked me out, I made it'?"

"No, I just knew she could use the money. So I tried to help."

"That simple?"

"That simple."

"Mom didn't like it."

"I know."

"And?"

"Well, if the situation was the same, I hope you'd help her

out every week—just like I did mine."

"Did you ever wish you had a brother or a sister?" I asked him.

"Sometimes—especially in the country."

"Because you were lonely?"

"No, to help me fight. See, if you walked down the road, and a white guy was comin' toward you, there wouldn't be no trouble. If you walked down the road by yourself with a friend, and there were two white guys walkin' toward you, there wouldn't be no trouble. If you were by yourself and there were two white guys, you better get ready to fight. If there were two of you and three of them, it was gonna be a fight. They were cowards. They only started somethin' if you were outnumbered. A brother would have helped even things out a little."

"Dad, if you could do things over, what would you do differently?"

For several seconds, he said nothing.

"You never thought about this?" I asked during the silence.

"No, I haven't. Why do you think I'm takin' so long? I really haven't given it much thought." He played with his coffee cup, and leaned back against the wall. "What would I do different . . . ?" he said to himself.

"Unreal," I thought to myself.

"Offhand, I can't think of nothin' I would do different. I kind of like the way I handled things."

"Nothing?"

"Not that I can think of. I always wanted kids. I always wanted my own business. When I started the restaurant, I told myself if it didn't work out, I could use the buildin' as a shoeshine parlor, and if that didn't work I could use it to keep supplies for a janitor service and clean office buildin's. So I had my bases covered if I struck out with the restaurant. I always tried to think things through. If this happens, then what? If that happens, then what?"

"That's it?"

"Wait, come to think of it, there is one thing."

I knew it. Financial decision. Personal decision. Should have married her and not her. Should have moved here and not there. Something he did or said that he wishes he could take back. Hell, doesn't he think he might have treated his own kids with more kindness—even if it was our fault for overreacting and for not understanding him better?

"I wish I had a little girl," he said.

"A little girl?"

"To a little girl, Daddy is everythin'. I'd love to walk in from work and have Daddy's little girl run up and kiss him sayin', 'Daddy's home!' Always wanted to know what that felt like."

"That's it?"

"But I'm happy with my three boys. Wouldn't send 'em back for anythin'."

"That's it?"

"All I can think of—and that one's kind of out of my hands." He laughed. "Yep, got no control over that."

"But what about decisions? You said you got divorced because the woman cheated on you. And you had a marriage annulled. You wouldn't have done those things again."

He leaned back again. The question, that way of thinking, was completely foreign to him. He shook his head again.

"You can't look at it like that. Ask yourself, would you a' done it if you thought it through? Did you learn anythin'? Okay, it didn't turn out the way I wanted it. What did you learn so you can make better decisions next time? The only way you're not goin' to make a mistake is if you don't do nothin'. If you get up out of bed and make decisions, some of them are guaranteed to turn out bad. So what are you goin' to do, stop gettin' out of bed?"

I nodded.

"What about you?" he asked. "Would you do things different?"

After that, what do you say? But I answered as honestly as I could. "Dad, we don't have time for all the things I would do differently."

"Well, that's too bad." He didn't ask me, "What things?" because, to him, it didn't matter.

"You can't be that hard on yourself 'cuz it'll affect the next one you make. Just try and think it through, do your best, make adjustments, and keep on steppin'."

15

SHIT HAPPENS, SO DEAL
WITH IT

"W hen are you gonna get married?" he asked.
"I told myself a long time ago I wouldn't get
married."

I remember standing in the kitchen at the old house feeling
smothered by the tension between Mom and Dad. But the biggest
reason for that vow is this: I never wanted any child of mine to
feel about their dad the way that I felt about mine.

"Oh, I've had girlfriends, especially one I met in college."

We were freshmen, and I already had a girlfriend in Los
Angeles. The girl I met in college had a boyfriend in Canada.
Fine. We agreed to be "just friends."

"What happened?" Dad asked.

"You really want to hear this?" He never asked me about my
love life, and it was the last thing I thought we'd be talking about.

"I do."

"Well, I had never met a black person from Canada."

"What do they call themselves," he laughed, "African-Cana-
dians?"

Her name was Phyllis. She spoke French and played folk

guitar. Short curly hair and light brown eyes. Perfect teeth. Never wore braces. She introduced me to Arlo Guthrie and I introduced her to the Four Tops. She taught me how to order in French and I taught her how to curse in English.

"Arlo Guthrie—any kin to Woody?"

I wouldn't have guessed that Dad knew that kind of music. "His son."

Dad nodded. He was really interested. He kept asking "Then what?" and "What did she say?" and "What did you do?"

I teased Phyllis for laughing at practically everything. I bet her I could crack her up just by holding up a number-two pencil. I put the pencil one inch from her face and stared at my watch. She laughed. Dad laughed.

"That's somethin' I'd do," he said.

The friendship even survived the summer—me in Los Angeles working a summer job at a gas station, her in Toronto on an internship with, I think, the United Way of Canada.

"Then what happened?"

We had been friends almost a year.

"Strictly platonic," I said.

She was sitting on the floor in my dorm room listening to music, and I was at my desk reading something.

"Larry, what do you want to do after college?"

"I don't know yet. Make some money."

"No, really. What do you want to do?"

"I want to make money."

"Are you serious?"

"'Course I'm serious."

"That's all?"

"That's all? That's hard enough."

"I mean, that's it?"

"Well, no."

"I didn't think so."

"I want to make lots of money."

Dad laughed.

"I laughed too, Dad, but she didn't."

'Oh, c'mon, she was jokin', right?"

No, she was not.

"Okay, Phyllis, what do you want to do when you graduate?"

"I want to help people."

"Well, I think that's great. So, you go help people, and I'll make money."

"Are you serious?"

"'Course, I'm serious."

"I can't, I can't believe—"

"Who doesn't want to make money?"

"I don't."

"Yeah, your father teaches philosophy at McGill, and my dad was a janitor who busted his ass and started a café. I shared a bedroom with one or both of my brothers until the tenth grade. Nobody's going to pay me to sit around and talk about existentialism. I want to make money."

"What's existentialism?" Dad asked.

"Well, it's kind of complicated. But it means there's no meaning or purpose behind the stuff that happens in your life—that your fate is in your own hands and that you have the power to determine the outcome of your life no matter your circumstances."

"You mean shit happens so deal with it."

"Ah, yeah, pretty much."

"How much tuition did we pay for that?" he laughed.

"Apparently, whatever it was, we overpaid."

"So what happened with Phyllis?" Dad asked.

"She told me I was shallow."

"Shallow?" Dad seemed baffled. "Because you wanted to make money?"

"Shallow and superficial."

He shook his head. "Maybe I didn't miss much by not goin' to college."

"You're right, Dad. You didn't miss much."

"What ever happened to your friend, you know, the basketball player?" Dad asked.

"You mean Perry?"

Perry and I met in the second grade. I didn't know until we were adults that his single mom was an alcoholic. His dad drove a bus, but I only saw him once. Perry was aggressive and angry.

"His home life was awful," I said.

In the fifth grade, our class picked the best kickball players for an annual game against the sixth grade class. Perry was the best kickball player in the class, but almost nobody voted him on the team. They hated him. When Perry played against the other students, he didn't just beat them. He taunted and ridiculed them.

When he pitched, he wouldn't just strike you out. He would announce the pitch, throw it, then laugh and deride the batter after he struck out.

"Sounds like Muhammad Ali," Dad laughed. "So the kids retaliated."

"Guess who they picked instead?"

"You?"

Despite my own doubts about my ability, the students had picked me as one of the starting players. So when class ended that day, I approached the teacher.

"I think it's unfair," I told her, "that Perry didn't make the team. He's the best player in the class, and I would like to give up my place for him."

"What did the teacher say?" Dad asked.

"She said, 'Okay, if you feel that strongly about it, he can play instead of you.'"

"Wish you had talked to me about it."

He said that Perry needed to learn that ability is one thing, but getting along with classmates is just as important in life. Ridiculing and belittling people will, at some point, get in your way. This could have been a very important lesson to him.

"Perry got what he deserved for treatin' his friends like shit. Now let's talk about you."

Dad folded his arms.

"You had a chance to play in the, what do you call it—kickball game—and you didn't take it. It opened up a door for you, and you should have walked through it. Are you sure you asked the teacher to let him take your place because you thought it was the right thing to do? Or because you didn't have any confidence in yourself?"

"A little of both."

"And it didn't do Perry any good."

He was right. The teacher started a pattern that persisted throughout Perry's elementary, junior high, and high school career. He got a pass—one of many until the end of high school.

He was far and away the best basketball player on the team. And there's a lot of pressure on high school coaches to win. But when it came to the practice sessions, he came late or not at all. Still, the coach played him.

One time Perry walked in late, and the coach chewed him out in front of his teammates. Perry took off his jersey, balled it up, and threw it in the coach's face. And Perry still started the game that evening.

"Ridiculous," Dad said.

The big colleges came to take a look at Perry. UCLA, Notre Dame, Marquette, USC, North Carolina, Duke. All of them.

He was that good.

But then they asked the coach about Perry's "head," his willingness to put the team first, his "coachability."

Now, a high school coach's currency is his credibility. So the coach did not lie. He told the big college recruiters of Perry's surliness, anger, and refusal to follow orders. He warned them that Perry was undisciplined, would disrupt their program, and become a "coach killer."

Bye-bye Notre Dame, bye-bye Marquette, bye-bye Duke, bye-bye all the major schools. All of the big schools—any of which Perry could have easily played for—refused to recruit him.

"Where'd he end up?" Dad said.

"Small college."

He knew he should have been at a first-tier school, not a small, undistinguished college where his skills could not improve, given the low level of competition. His attitude remained defiant, and he failed to attract attention to "move up" from his small school to a major college. He started showing up to practice even later, smoking dope, and cutting classes. Soon his coach, despite the pressure to win, kicked him off the team. Then he dropped out.

Dad shook his head. "Well, he still could have made the best of his situation. And didn't. What's he doin' now?"

"Lives in the back room in his mom's house. Same bedroom since the second grade."

"Hm-m-m, as bad as his situation was with his mom and dad, there's always somebody who has it worse off. It still comes down to you—how you deal with it."

We sat in silence for a little while. It was oddly comfortable.

"How's your other friend doin', the one you went all the way through school with?"

"Frank has a problem."

"What do you mean?"

Frank's father worked construction, and one day came home and announced that he simply couldn't take work anymore. At first, the family assumed he'd just had a bad day. But it quickly became obvious that there was something seriously wrong.

He refused to leave the house, started speaking to himself, and became increasingly detached.

"What do you mean, 'detached'?"

The family might be eating dinner, and suddenly Frank's dad would start talking about a car he owned years ago. Several therapists examined him, and could not come up with anything physically wrong with him. He had a breakdown from which he never recovered.

Despite his father's illness, Frank became a lawyer, one of his brothers an engineer, another a veterinarian. But then Frank started doing drugs.

"He's lost jobs and I don't know what will happen to him. Frank, I think, could never deal with his father's condition."

"He has two brothers, right?"

"That's true."

"Same household? Same mother, right?"

"Yes."

"His brothers turned out all right. At some point, you have to take responsibility. There's a sayin': If you want your prayers answered, you'd better get up off your knees and do somethin' about it. So, no, I'm not buyin' it. No matter how bad things are, you have a responsibility to try. Don't mean you will. If people see that you're tryin', you'll be surprised at how much help you'll get."

I thought about what Dad just said. "Do you know why I ended up going to an Ivy League school?" I asked him.

"No. Don't think you ever said."

"Two reasons. Mr. Katzman. And Mrs. Workman."

My high school government teacher, Howard Katzman, praised me as the only student in his career to make A's on all his tests. One day, walking down the classroom aisles passing out material, he asked me what I was reading.

"A college guide," I said.

"What schools are you looking at?"

I had been focusing on a Midwest school with "rolling admissions." This meant that January high school graduates could start that school in February, rather than wait until the fall, the policy of most four-year colleges and universities.

"That's a dumb reason to pick a school," he said. "Besides, you can do much better than that one. Why not the Ivys?"

I didn't know Ivy League from bush league. I would be the first college grad in my family, and had only one uncle with a four-year degree. I had no clue how it worked. Mr. Katzman insisted that I think more seriously about where I should go and why.

I stayed late at school one evening. The school counselor, Mrs. Workman, was walking down the hall.

"Larry, have you signed up to take the SAT?" she asked.

"What's that?"

"It's an aptitude test that colleges use. Do well and your name goes on a list that schools use to recruit good students."

"How much does the test cost?"

"It's free. They're giving it to certain inner-city schools. Ours is one."

I took it, got placed on some list, and started receiving college catalogues almost everyday in the mail for months. Yale, Harvard, Stanford, UCLA . . . .

One catalogue was from Brown. I decided to apply there for early decision, and was accepted. The school gave me a generous financial aid package.

"No Mr. Katzman, no Mrs. Workman, who knows?" I told Dad. "I completely lucked out."

"Wait a second. You know, the harder you work, the luckier you get. If you hadn't been about somethin', none of that would have happened. Someone can open a door, but you have to have sense enough to jump through."

It was 7:05.

16

GOOD FRIENDS

"Why don't you have friends?"

How can someone have no one to go places with, no one to talk to, no one to help work out problems, no one to share ideas, no one just to relax around and do nothing. How is that possible? How could he be happy?

"I've always been a loner," he said.

"I know, but why?"

"Only child, I guess. Always been on my own. And it's hard to find a good friend. A real one. You're lucky if you can find one or two. If you think you have more than that, your judgment's bad."

"So, Mom has bad judgment?"

"You said that," he laughed. "I didn't."

My mother's friends were interesting and positive, full of "piss and vinegar" as Mom said. Each one had something special. Along with friends, she had loads of relatives—uncles, cousins, nieces, and nephews—more than enough to make up for Dad's none.

"I think you're wrong about that one, Dad."

When Mom found a friend, she kept her. But she didn't

make friends easily. That was certainly the case with Mrs. Jeffries.

When I went away to college, only one other kid from my high school also went, Frank Jeffries. I didn't know him well in high school. We had a couple of mutual friends, but that was about it. I'd heard he got accepted to my college, and I was hoping he would go somewhere else.

"Why?" Dad asked, "Wouldn't you want someone from your same high school goin' to your college? Goin' off to a new place—you'd be there with somebody you know."

No, part of the point in going to school far away is to reinvent yourself. It took a while to learn that everybody feels that way. In my case, I was shy—too shy. College provided me a chance to start over in a new school and transform myself into someone more confident and assertive. But with Frank there, he'd know "the new me" was a performance.

Frank and I did become friends. He always encouraged me when I hit a tough spot in the classroom. He predicted greater things for me than I did.

"You got the talent," he'd say.

I insisted that he had more. We even debated the issue.

"This is a pretty stupid thing to debate don't you think?" I said in the middle of it. "What happens if I win?"

He taught me about jazz, Impressionist painters, and salt-water fish. He had studied math, chemistry, biology, and French. I called him "The Renaissance Man" and said he was born in the wrong century and the wrong country.

We debated politics and, when he took a course in economics, I started losing more arguments than usual. So I took economics to try to even things up.

I learned about the damage done by minimum-wage laws, the cost of unnecessary regulations on business, and that competition results in better-quality and lower-priced goods—the same things my Dad had always said, in his simpler fashion.

"And I never took no economics," Dad said, laughing.

"No, you just practiced it."

One evening, Frank and I were sitting on the floor of his dorm room listening to music.

"Frank, do you have any brothers or sisters?"

"Yes, I have two brothers."

"So do I. Where do you fit—oldest, youngest?"

"I'm in the middle," he said.

"So am I."

"What's your birthday?" he asked.

"April 27. Yours?"

"April 24."

We just looked at each other. "Wow." I don't know why we'd never asked each other these questions.

His younger brother was only a couple of months older than Dennis, and his older brother was born in the same year as Kirk.

"Where are you parents from?" I asked.

"Alabama."

"My mother is from Alabama, my Dad from Georgia."

"What town in Alabama?" Frank asked.

"Huntsville."

"Mine are from Selma."

Frank's parents relocated to California the same year mine did.

"Did either of your parents go to college?" I asked.

"My mother did. She spent two years in a small black college, but I doubt you've ever heard of it."

"What's it called?

"Talladega."

"Frank, Frank . . . my mom went to Talladega."

We found that our mothers were there at the same time, but

didn't know each other.

When we came home for the summers and for Christmas vacation, I got to know Frank's mother. She was smart, curious, and pleasant. When I first met her, she was sitting on the couch reading a large photo book.

"What are you reading, Mrs. Jeffries?"

"A book on Egypt."

"Oh, are you going?"

"No," she said, "Egypt just fascinates me."

I knew Mom would like her, and for almost two years Frank and I tried get them to meet each other.

"Oh, no, Larry, I don't really feel like having her over," Mom said.

"Oh, Frank, I don't know that I have time for company," Frank's mom told him.

Finally I bought two tickets for *The Godfather*. I knew my mother would like it. It was about a man who kicks ass. Her kind of guy.

"Here. These are for you and Mrs. Jeffries. They are not refundable. You two figure out the arrangements."

From that point on, they became close friends. They went out together, worried about their boys together, and consoled each other when things went wrong.

"I didn't know how your mother and Ruth met," Dad said. "All those things you and Frank have in common. Well, I'll say."

"And Mrs. Jeffries always asked about you, what you were up to, questions about the café."

"Really? I had no idea. I thought Mom's friends were against me."

It wasn't true. Mom's friends respected Dad perhaps more than Mom did.

"You didn't play around. You came home like clockwork. No

drinking, no gambling. Careful with your money. That's a lot. I heard her friends talking about it."

"I had no idea," he said. "No idea."

When the phone rang—before my brothers and I had social lives—it was always for Mom. Not one time did anyone call and ask for my father. No one ever visited him.

"Don't you get lonely?" I asked Dad.

"Sometimes. Sometimes. My friends are right here, right here at this place." He tapped on the counter, "Right here."

My mother's friends were so colorful, each one uniquely different. But with all the people in our neighborhood, including the parents of our friends, she rarely befriended any of them. So if my mother liked someone enough for her to drop by—especially without calling first—she had to be special.

"Hello, is Vi there?"

I never had to ask who was calling—I could tell Mom's friends apart by their distinctive voices.

"Mom, Cee is on the phone."

Cee was one of my favorites. She walked with a hop, always upbeat and seemingly eager to see us. Cee was "light-skinned," about the color of my mother. She chewed gum, the only adult I ever saw who did. She wore colorful dresses and talked about the things she and her husband did. She talked about her husband as if they were friends. They traveled. She cared about what he thought. She loved the things he said that made her laugh. It was such a contrast with how my mother talked about my father. Cee, my mother told me, had no children.

"Larry," she'd ask, "how is school? What are you learning? What's your favorite subject?"

She always brought Doublemint gum.

"Cee," we'd ask, "do you have any gum?" As she spoke to Mom, she'd reach into her purse without pausing, and pull some out. She never came unprepared. Kirk and Dennis would come in, say a few things so they wouldn't appear rude, grab their stick of gum and leave. I would stay. I enjoyed watching Cee and my mother talk because Mom acted so differently around her. Mom loosened up around her.

Cee, like Mom, had a big, honest laugh and she made my mother laugh, even on the phone. They both sewed much of their own clothing, and they talked about fabrics, how much they cost, where to get what on sale, what Jackie Kennedy was wearing, and their favorite Dodger, Duke Snider.

They talked about "home." They were from the same "part of the country"—Huntsville, Alabama—and always said that "some day, when the time was right," they were going back home.

Mom once heard me playing a song about a man who missed the South. She stopped in the doorway to listen.

"Who's singing that song?"

"Jr. Walker and the All-Stars," I said. "It's called 'Way Back Home.'"

> Oh, there's good 'n bad things
> About the South, boy
> Oh, and some leave a bitter taste
> In my mouth, now
> Like the black man livin' across the track
> White man were on the other side
> Holdin' him back
> Way back home, now
>
> Oh, but we won't talk about that
> 'Cause it's understood
> Ev'rybody sees the bad
> But what about the good?
> Ooh, I'd give anything
> Just to smell that scent
> Of honeysuckle growin'

On a backyard fence
Way back home, now
I'd love to smell the wetness
Of grass and trees
And see ground kissed
By honey bees
Like way back home, now

Oh, but childhood days
Are dead 'n gone
Well, but the memories
Still linger on
Oh, have you ever gone swimmin'
In a muddy creek
With nothin' on your body
From head to feet?
Way back home, yeah

How you play for the game
Like hide an seek
Yeah!
And snake through the weeds
Overhear the streams
Well, I know some kids
Still play those games
But when they play
It just ain't the same
Like way back home

Oh, I really miss those things
That have faded away
I remember them
Like it was yesterday
Now, way back home

"It sure reminds me of home," Mom said.

"I didn't feel that way at all about the country," Dad said. "I hated it. Couldn't wait to get out. No-o-o-o-o desire to go back."

But Mom and Cee always talked about cousin so-and-so or aunt so-and-so "down in the country." I used to think that Cee and Mom were cousins. I liked thinking that I was related to Cee and I was afraid, if I asked Mom about it, she would say "no." So I never asked. But I decided on my own that she "was family."

"Cee always asked about you, Dad."

"Really? I didn't think she cared about me one way or the other."

No, Cee always asked about my father, "Ran," she called him. My mother would grunt a response and turn the conversation back to people they knew "down home." I never knew what Cee or her husband did for a living. I came to learn that my mother rarely discussed what people did if they had "regular ol' jobs," as my mother put it—meaning hands-on jobs like housekeeping, valet, janitor work, or bus driving.

My favorite friend of my mother's was "Aunt" Dorothy. Dad couldn't stand her. Whenever he spoke of her, he called her "Jones," her last name. That irritated Mom.

I adored her and would sometimes tell her things I wouldn't dream about telling Mom. Dorothy always encouraged me and told me how special I was. She even went to our Little League games and told me that I had ability.

Dorothy was funny and loving—all three hundred pounds of her.

"I like to eat," she said. Her doctor warned her, and she vowed to watch her weight, but never stuck to it.

She was incredibly smart and well read. She was the first person I ever heard use the word "echelon," and she was interested in national and international politics. She and Mom would talk about the latest *Time* magazine cover story.

She worked at a place that made mannequins, and said she liked her job. She once took Dennis and me to her workplace, and we watched her assemble arms, heads, and torsos. As she finished each mannequin, Dennis and I gave the freakishly rigid, naked, bald, life-sized dolls names. I couldn't imagine that someone as bright as Dorothy could attach limbs and bodies all day without going crazy.

"I'm just doing this while I work my way through med school," she said.

Dorothy always knew what was going on, even when Mom was a couple of steps behind. Once, when I was in high school, Dorothy and Mom were talking in the back room.

"Mom, could I borrow the car keys? I asked.

"Where are you going?" Dorothy wanted to know.

"A date."

Where?" she asked.

"Bowling alley."

"Then stop by the drug store," she said.

"It's not that kind of date," I said.

"Stop by the drug store anyway," said Dorothy, "you never know."

"Dorothy, I'm going bowling."

"You never know."

"I don't have that kind of luck."

"Tonight might be the night."

"Okay," I said.

"The drug store?" said Mom. "Why would he stop by the drug store? He's going to the bowling alley."

"Jesus, Mom."

In 1965, Mom, Kirk, Dennis, Dorothy, and I took a trip up California's Highway One in the old Rambler. The Watts riots had started, and it was surreal heading up north and watching military trucks in green camouflage heading south on the other side of the highway. I guess it was a good time to be out of the city. We went to Sacramento, San Francisco, Yosemite National Park, and Hearst Castle. Mom told me about William Randolph Hearst and yellow journalism, and that the movie *Citizen Kane* was based on his life.

It was a great trip. We even took in a Dodgers-Giants game at Candlestick Park and listened to the ballgames on the radio. Mom corrected legendary Dodger broadcaster Vin Scully's grammar.

"Back, back, and wa-a-ay back. To the wall! A home run for Willie McCovey. And if it weren't for the wind, there's no telling where that ball would have went."

"Would have gone!" Mom said, shaking her head.

Dorothy kept up a continuous comedy monologue. After walking around Yosemite, we sat down at a rest area. A bald man with skinny white legs and wearing a massive pair of Bermuda shorts sat down nearby—luckily, just out of earshot.

"Look at that man," Dorothy said. "Look at that ugly man. Good Lord, that is one ugly man. Ain't no reason for anybody to be that ugly."

"Dorothy!" Mom said. We were howling.

"Now just be honest, Vi, ain't no reason for anybody to be that ugly." Even Mom started laughing.

When Mom and Dorothy weren't talking politics, they talked about men—as in how useless they thought they were and that they "just took up space."

"Dorothy," I once asked, "why haven't you gotten married?"

"Honey, if you could take the best qualities from all my sisters' husbands, and put them in one man, you'd still come up short."

Dad would overhear them talking, and their voices would die down when he walked by them. He assumed that he was likely the topic of conversation. Dad could only imagine the digs Dorothy must have made at him, given the harsh things he'd heard her say about other men.

Dorothy helped me pack for law school. She waited for Mom to leave the room.

"I know your mother says all sorts of bad things about your father. But you should know this: He was always there."

"What do you mean?" I asked.

"He worked and he came home. He was dependable. Kept his word. He kept up his end of the bargain, no matter what your mother says. He was always there."

"Dorothy said that?" Dad said, shocked.

"She sure did."

"I had no idea she felt like that."

"That's what she said, 'He was always there.'"

"'He was always there.' She said that?"

"You guys make quite a pair—you and Mom." I added, "She is one tough hombre."

17

"SHE'S SOMETHING"

I got a paper route delivering the *Herald Examiner* on my black Schwinn bicycle. George was the man in charge of all the delivery boys. He was balding on top with thick white hair on the sides and reeked of cigar smoke from the stogies he was never without.

"You're late, Elder," he barked, no matter what time you came in. After the first time he said it, you realized it was his way of saying hello. "What is this world coming to?"

"Be glad I'm here," I said. "Let's see you try and deliver them."

"Hey Hal, a lady complained that you hit her dog with the paper. What is this world coming to? You're fired." Everybody got fired at least once a month.

George always complained about "what this world is coming to." I delivered during the murder spree of Richard Speck, the serial killer who raped and butchered eight Chicago student nurses. Each day brought new revelations.

"Oh, Sweet Jesus," George threw up his hands. "Don't put me on the jury. I'll tell you what they should do to this bastard. Cut off one body part each day. Then give him a trial. Coleman, you're late! Yeah, one body part for every nurse he killed. What is this world coming to?"

George stacked the number of newspapers each boy needed for his route. We picked each paper up, one at a time, folded it, and put it in a machine that had a mechanical arm with string attached to it. When the paper touched the arm, it came down and then up, leaving the paper neatly folded in half with a tight string bow around it. Once you got the hang of it, the whole thing took about a second. You had to be careful not to get your finger caught under the arm. It wouldn't rip off a finger, but it could gouge and tear into one. Then you scooped up the papers and put them in a canvas bag, which fit over your bike handlebars.

"It was a good job," said Dad, "except when it came to gettin' paid."

My first route had thirty houses, and I did so well I soon got a bigger one, this time with almost fifty houses. We had to knock on the door to collect from each customer every month. Most paid on time, and you were paid a percentage of your expected collections. But if someone was late or you got completely stiffed, it came out of the paperboy's end.

"Mom always thought that was unfair, and she wondered whether it was the *Herald Examiner's* policy or George's," I told Dad.

Every month, no matter how successful I was in collecting on time and from almost every customer on my route, George always said I was short.

"Elder, you owe me three dollars."

"But George—"

"It's right here."

"But I was really careful—-"

"No you weren't." He punched a bunch of keys on his adding machine, looked at the tape and chomped down on his cigar.

"Hu-umm, yup, you're three dollars light."

George did this every month to every kid.

"So I told Mom."

"Uh-oh," Dad laughed.

She asked me how much I kept and how much George got, and then she went over my account records for every month I worked.

"All right," she said. "Let's go."

While she drove there, she asked me to tell her about George, what I knew about him, and what he was like. When Mom and I got to his office, the place was jammed with kids and the sound of two dozen mechanical arms going up and down. Everything went quiet, like the Tombstone saloon just before a gunfight. The kids stared at Mom standing in the door with her arms on her hips, and me pointing my arm toward George. He looked up and saw her stomping right toward him.

"Now, Dad, you know how she walks when she's mad."

"Oh, I know."

Before Mom even got to George's desk, he mashed out the cigar, reached into the drawer, pulled out a stack of bills and started counting bills off into a pile.

"Never said anything to Mom, just started counting. She scooped up the money and said, 'Don't you try that again. What is this world coming to?'"

I came home twenty-three dollars richer.

Dad laughed, leaned back, and clapped his hands.

"Wait, there's a little more to this."

I told Dad that when she and I laughed about this years later, Mom regretted how she handled it.

"Why?" Dad said. "She handled it just fine."

"Not what she thought. She said, 'I wish I had that to do all over again. That man was cheating all you kids. I should have gotten everybody's money straight.'"

"She's somethin'," Dad said.

"Well, she didn't pull out a gun like you did on the ice man."

"Whatever works."

"Did you know Mom is why Dennis joined the Army?"

"What do you mean?"

Dennis was just bopping around. He dropped out of high school, started doing drugs, got clean, then started up again. She tried everything. She helped him find jobs, but he wouldn't keep them. She paid for a school extension course, but he stopped going after a short time.

"Mom was desperate. I don't know how, but she finally convinced him to go into the Army," I told Dad. "Maybe Dennis agreed because he thought they wouldn't take him."

Dennis applied, passed his mental and physical tests, and it looked like a go. But there was a problem. The local recruiter refused to sign the necessary papers.

"Dennis told Mom that the recruiter wouldn't sign."

This was during the Vietnam War. If they put a mirror under your nose, and you could fog it up just a little, you were in—especially if you wanted in. But this recruiter refused, and Dennis couldn't explain why. Mom got the recruiter's name, went to his office, and begged him.

"Why won't you sign this?" she said, pointing to the papers she'd laid on his desk.

"He's too light. Doesn't weigh enough for his height."

"How light?"

"Two pounds."

"You're kidding."

"Ma'am, regulations are regulations."

He barely looked at her. When he wasn't running his hand back and forth over his crew cut, he straightened his desk and looked at his watch.

"He acted like I was some kind of gnat on his ass," she told me later.

They went back and forth. Under her grilling, he admitted that he did have the authority to waive the weight shortfall and admit Dennis.

"But I just don't like his attitude," he said.

"Is that it?" Mom said. "You could sign for him, but you just won't?"

"That's right," the recruiter said. "He has to go through me, and I say no."

Mom couldn't remember when she was that angry. In front of Dennis was the possibility that he might learn some discipline, get some direction, and maybe even make a career out of the Army.

"That recruiter liked lording over me," Mom told me. "And I wasn't having it."

She got up and closed his door.

"Here's how this is going to go." She picked up Dennis's papers and put them in front of the recruiter.

"You're going to sign these right now."

"No, I won't."

"Oh, yes, you will. If you don't, this is what I'm going to do."

Mom grabbed the collar on her blouse.

"I'm going to rip off this top. And I'm going to run out of your office screaming at the top of my lungs that you tried to rape me."

"You'll do no such thing! I'll deny it! And nobody's going to believe you!"

"Most won't. But enough of them will."

She pointed to the other offices through the glass panels and to the people walking around.

"If you're the asshole I think you are, I bet you've made some enemies. And they won't care whether it's true or not, they'll put in your record that you were accused of rape—and there'll be an investigation. Doesn't matter how it turns out."

"You, you—"

"And your enemies will use it against you. It's your word against mine. My son is headed for jail or the cemetery if he doesn't turn his life around. Now I know you don't give a shit. But that's my son. And I do give a shit. And this is his shot. And I'll be damned if I let you get in my way."

"You won't do that!"

"Try me!"

"Don't tell me," Dad said.

He signed the papers.

"Now get out!" he said.

"And don't you try anything," Mom said, "or I'll be back."

Dennis didn't make a career out of the Army, but he served and was honorably discharged.

"Did she think about this whole plan ahead of time?" Dad asked.

"That's what I asked her," I said. "She told me she improvised."

"She's a pistol," he said.

"I have a saying about Mom."

"What?"

"If she'd gone into politics, she would have been president. She had gone into crime, she would have been Charlie Manson."

"My goodness."

She wasn't big on giving compliments, and even worse at accepting them.

"Mom, that's a beautiful blouse."

"Oh, this old thing."

Or, "Mom, did you make that? It's beautiful."

"Yeah, but I made a mistake here and here."

Or, "Mom your hair looks great."

"What? I barely combed it, and the ends need cutting."

One day when it happened, I said, "Mom, when someone gives you a compliment, I want you to try something."

"What?" she said.

"Try 'Thank you.'"

"After that," Dad asked, "did she get any better?"

"No."

"Didn't think so."

"I don't know what it's like to be married to her, but she's helluva mother."

Mom made me feel like I could spit lightening and make bullets bounce off my chest. She sat me down on the front porch when I was about six years old. She had an illustrated book of all the presidents from George Washington to then-President Dwight Eisenhower. We talked about their achievements and disappointments.

"Larry," she said tapping the book, "if you work hard enough and want it bad enough, someday you can be in this book."

"She's right," Dad said.

"All I know is that I thought if she believed it, it must be true."

"It is."

And no one could make you feel worse.

"I was goofing off instead of studying for the Ohio bar exam," I told Dad.

I spent very little time on it, never went to the bar review classes, and assumed anyone getting through a good law school could handle this test. After all, an 80 or 90 percent passing margin? How hard could it be?

About a week before the exam, a friend brought over a practice test he'd gotten from his bar review course.

"I took the practice exam myself. I flunked it big time. It was much harder than I thought. And I only had a week to learn what bar review courses cover in four months."

I already had a job at a major law firm, and they damn well expect you to pass the bar. Your career is damaged before it starts if you flunk.

"What did you do?"

"I studied my ass off, but deep down I knew it was way too late."

I called Mom, told her what happened, and prepared her for my imminent failure.

"Mom," I said, "I'm so sorry I let you down."

She said nothing for a long time. "No, Larry, you let yourself down."

"Ouch," Dad said. "What happened?

"I passed. But I never pulled a stunt like that again. You remember when I came home to take the California bar exam?"

"Not really."

"It's one of the toughest bar exams in the country with a high failure rate. I took a long vacation from work, flew out to California, closed the bedroom door, and studied for three weeks. Do you remember what you said?"

"No."

"It's a three-day exam. I came home after the first day and told Mom that it wasn't hard. 'If that's all it is,' I said, 'I'll breeze through.' Then I noticed you sitting there, and I thought you were going to jump on me for being arrogant. So I said, 'But I guess I better not get over-confidant.' Do you remember what you said?"

"No."

"Well, I do. You said, 'If you don't believe in yourself, who will?' I was shocked. I thought, 'He's actually encouraging me.'"

"I've always encouraged you—or tried to."

I thought I'd leave that alone—for now.

It was 8:10.

18

"NOT AS TOUGH AS YOU THINK"

D oris, a nineteen-year-old college student from Tennessee, moved in and lived with us for a few years. Her mother grew up in Huntsville and was a childhood friend of my mother's. The friend asked Mom if she could help Doris when she came to L.A. for college. Mom offered to let her stay with us until she graduated.

We picked her up from the airport. What would she be like? How would she look?

"I'm Doris. You must be Mrs. Elder."

"Call me Vi." Mom said. Mom liked her right away.

Doris glowed—beautiful, sophisticated, and smart. She couldn't wait to discover and conquer Los Angeles, quite a contrast from her Tennessee hometown. Our house had a different energy from the moment she walked in.

"I hope that girl doesn't get hurt," I once heard Mom say to Dorothy.

"Better watch out for that girl," Dorothy said, "and maybe she'll get through."

Doris sang all the time—when she was doing laundry, shopping, playing gin rummy, or brushing her hair. She sounded as good as the singers whose records she danced to. She danced well, and taught us the latest steps—or at least tried to.

We'd watch her try on and discard dress after dress until she found the one that worked. I could never predict the one she'd settle on. Then she'd carefully pick out the earrings.

"This one or this one?"

"That one," I'd say.

"No, too flashy."

"How about this one?"

"No. Don't like that one. Yeah, I'm going to go with this one."

She never agreed with any of my choices, but at least she asked.

She sang Shirley Bassey's "You Put A Spell On Me" while she put on lipstick and misted her wrists with perfume.

She was riveting. We'd listen to her speak with friends on the phone. The way she laughed, smelled, and acted created a whole new world in this nearly all-male household. And Mom liked having her companionship.

Nobody complained when Mom moved Kirk back into the bedroom with Dennis and me. So once again we triple-bunked. We loved having a "sister." When we had girl trouble, she'd give advice.

A date would show up, and sit nervously in the living room as he waited for her to make an entrance. I'd talk with them, and try to guess whether they would be granted a second date. I liked many of them, but never saw any of them again. One date and out.

"If that's Richard, don't tell him I'm here," she'd say.

"What's wrong with him?"

"Oh, you know."

"What?"

"Just, you know. Didn't work."

"Why didn't it?"

"Just didn't."

Were girls going to be this brutal when I started dating?

Eventually, the rejects would stop calling. I felt sorry for them. One prospect was a Marine. He showed up in his blue uniform and wore the shiniest black shoes I'd ever seen. He brought flowers, gave us candy, and stood up when Mom walked into the room. Never saw him again.

Doris's closet was stacked with boxes and boxes of shoes. The piles were so high you could almost hide behind them. She wouldn't be able see you—but you could see her.

That gave me an idea.

Doris always got dressed in the closet. I could hide in her closet, cover myself with the boxes and take a peek at her as she dressed.

I buried myself in shoes and boxes, and waited for her to come out of the shower. In a few minutes, the door opened. I was scared to death, afraid to even breathe. I shut my eyes, held my breath, and tried not to even let my pores open. After what seemed like forever, she dressed, cut off the light, and left. I never "saw" her and never tried again.

"What did you see? Tell me!" Kirk demanded.

"No, I chickened out. Kept my eyes closed."

"That's just sad. You're never going to get anywhere in life. And I'm too big to try it," he said.

At last, one of Doris's dates made the cut. Don was tall, well-built, and GQ handsome. Doris was crazy about him. All the girls on the street managed to be outside right about the time Don pulled up in his big, shiny white car without a speck of dust. He was kind to Kirk and Dennis and me, too. He took us swimming and to Dodger games. He spent time talking and laughing with us, a big contrast with Doris's other dates who thought of us as impediments. Sometimes he wore tight shirts or pants that showed muscles upon muscles.

"Honey, that is a man," Doris said to a girlfriend.

Mom despised him. Absolutely, positively, couldn't stand the man.

One time, I said something about Don being handsome.

"You think so?" Mom said.

"Of course he's handsome. His face, his body, perfect teeth."

"Well, I don't see it."

"You don't see it?"

"No."

"Mom, you just don't like him. And when you don't like somebody they could look like Sidney Poitier and you'll think he's ugly."

"Hu-u-um, maybe so. But there's something about that man."

"What?"

"I don't know, but there's something I don't like."

"Thought so."

"Don't tell Doris," she said. "It's her life, but I'll tell you right now something's not right about that man. If I'm wrong, may I be struck by lightning."

"Oh, Mom." I cupped my hands and clapped them, imitating the sound of thunder.

"You just wait," she said.

One day, a few months later, Doris came home, rushed in, and dove onto the couch. She cried for hours. Don, she discovered, was not only married, but had two children. His wife found out about Doris and confronted her in the department store where Doris worked part-time. Doris was crushed and humiliated.

Mom put her arms around Doris. They sat rocking for hours. Doris moved away about three years later, but she was never the same—no longer the joyful co-ed who bounded down from the plane that day.

"So that's what happened to Don," Dad said. "He was just gone one day. And nobody told me what happened."

"Mom smelled a rat from the get-go."

"Like I said. She's a pistol."

"More like an Uzi."

"What's an Uzi?"

"An Israeli combat submachine gun."

He almost spilled his coffee.

"Better not have an affair if you want to live," I said.

"Don't worry."

When Mom stopped working at the restaurant, she took a job as a clerk with the phone company. After a few years, Pacific Telephone considered her for a supervisor position, a huge deal and rare opportunity for a clerk with no four-year degree, in a facility with no black supervisors.

She underwent a series of tests. And came home every night on the verge of pulling out.

"I don't think I can pass these tests," she said. "I think I'm cracking up."

But she studied hard and passed.

Then there were months of training. She again came home stressed and wondering whether she could make it.

"I'm going in tomorrow and tell them I can't do it," she said more than once. "I want to go back to my old job."

But she hung in and made supervisor. They gave her an office and an assistant.

"Your father found out how much money I was making," she said, smiling, a few months later.

They never discussed money. But Mom needed Dad to know that she made more money than he did.

"How did he find out?"

"I left my paycheck on the kitchen table when he was drinking his coffee, and I got up to use the bathroom and pretended that I forgot it."

"How do you know he looked at it?"

"Well, I put the envelope right here."

She demonstrated how she carefully placed it between "these two marks."

"Then I went to the bathroom, and when I came back I could tell it had been moved because it wasn't on the same marks."

She couldn't have been happier.

I didn't tell Dad about the paycheck, the marks on the table, and Mom's glee.

When I went away to college, I found out that a lot of parents tried to stop their kids from going away to school. Some tried hard to get them to stay local.

"It's a good thing Mom wasn't like that." She looked forward to my seeing another part of the country. "She didn't feel a thing when I left."

"Oh, yes she did."

"What do you mean?"

"Remember when she dropped you off at the airport?"

"Yes."

"Came home and threw up all night."

"Really?"

"I know. I was there to help her up. And I was depressed for days."

"Really?"

"We're not as tough as you think."

"You know, Mom ran off one of Kirk's girlfriends."

"What?"

Kirk was about seventeen, and was seeing a woman who was

in her mid-twenties with a kid.

"Mom was not happy."

"I don't blame her," Dad said.

She was originally from San Jose and told Kirk she wanted to move back there with him as soon as they could get together the money to travel.

"Mom sat her down and told her it was unfair to push this kind of responsibility on a seventeen-year-old still in high school. She offered to pay for her bus fare to San Jose, and give her a couple hundred dollars to get on her feet. But she was not to see or call Kirk ever again."

"What happened?"

"She took the money, and Kirk never saw her again."

"Damn."

She didn't do quite the same thing to me, but she made it clear when she didn't think someone was suitable.

"I brought a girl I met in law school out to L.A. during a semester break. Mom immediately disliked her."

"Why?"

"Mom told me she talked too much."

The three of us were at home, standing in the hallway, when Mom saw a spider on the wall directly behind the girl.

"Quick," Mom said to her, "hand me your shoe."

Startled, she removed her shoe. Thwack! Mom smashed the spider with the shoe—and handed the shoe back to her.

"With the spider on the bottom?"

"She didn't even wipe the shoe off."

"No."

"Yes."

Dad smiled. "I don't know what to say."

"Neither did the girl."

We both laughed.

19

WAY BACK HOME

"What was it like," Dad asked, "goin' down to Huntsville, comin' from a big city like this?"

Every summer for three years, my brothers and I took a train to "the family farm" in a tiny town called Toney, right outside Huntsville, Alabama, where my mother, her sister, and brothers were raised. I was nine or ten the first time.

Going from Los Angeles to Huntsville was like stepping into a prehistoric era. Grandma and Grandpa didn't have indoor plumbing. The restroom was an outhouse a hundred yards from the house. At night, my grandparents set a bucket with vinegar near your bed.

"That's in case y'all got to pee in the middle of night," said Grandpa.

If you had a more serious emergency, you grabbed a roll of toilet paper, and groped your way in the darkness toward the outhouse by following the God-awful smell.

My grandparents scolded us for using so much toilet paper to wipe ourselves. A roll might last them more than a month, and Grandma asked why it was necessary for us to be so "city clean."

"Ain't nobody goin' smell you down there, no way."

To bathe, they pumped water from the well in large buckets. The buckets were hung on a rod over the fireplace. The heated water was poured into a large bathing tub. Kirk went first and enjoyed fresh, fairly hot water. Then it was my turn to wash up in the now warmish, dirty water.

"Hurry up, Larry," Dennis said. "Grandma, he's taking his time on purpose."

After I got out, Dennis balked, "Grandma, the water is nasty."

"Why don't cha just stand outside, then, an' shake the dirt off?" Grandma said. "Boy, git in that tub!"

He complied. After this, we started bathing in the creek. The water was cold, but it looked cleaner.

Grandpa was tall and strong. From the moment he woke up until he went to bed, he was never without a pipe. All day, he reached into his blue overalls, and carefully opened a packet of coiled tobacco. He broke off a piece and stuffed it in his pipe just as the last wad was burning out. He bent down next to the fireplace, grabbed a straw, stuck it in the fire and lit the pipe. He mashed down the red-hot tobacco with a finger that was blackened with ashes.

He was a thing of beauty. I couldn't take my eyes off of him.

"Whatcha lookin' at?" he said when he caught me staring.

He hummed, always, no matter what he was doing. He hummed when he checked the chickens for eggs. He hummed when he fed the hogs. He hummed when he grabbed a stick and tried to kill a snake that Dennis saw in the front of the old three-bedroom farmhouse.

He joked all the time, and they all started with, "Did ah ever tell you 'bout the time. . ." That's how he began the first joke he told me, just moments after I'd laid eyes on him for the first time.

"Did ah ever tell you 'bout the man who said, 'If I had some ham, I'd make me some ham and eggs—if I had the eggs.'"

He told me that Mom was so difficult to make laugh that he would use her to test out the jokes he planned to tell at his Mason meetings.

"If that girl laughed, then I knowed it was a good 'un."

Grandpa never cursed. When he dropped the bucket after he just milked the cows, he said, "Oh, foot!" When he checked the nest of a laying hen, and found that she had underperformed, he said, "Oh, foot."

"What did you say, Grandpa?" I finally had to ask.

"Oh, foot!"

"Excuse me?"

"Oh, foot."

"How do you spell it?"

"Spell what?"

"Whatever it was you said."

"I ain't spellin'. I'm speakin'."

He walked slowly, a kind of shuffle that had less to do with age and more about "not seein' no point in rushin' 'round all the time."

"I'll git there when I git there," he'd say.

He drove their 1949 car with the gearshift on the steering column the same way he walked—slowly. Fifteen miles per hour, at the most. He and Grandma occasionally waved to people and gossiped about them as they drove.

They passed a middle-aged man in a straw hat with a goofy, toothless smile. He was sitting on a tree stump and puffing a pipe.

"Yonder go John Lesley." Grandma waved. "Looks like he's stayin' with Freddie tonight."

"Been there all week," Grandpa said.

"*That's* John Lesley?" I asked.

"How'd you know him?" Grandma asked.

I told her that when we did something Mom thought stupid, she'd say, "John Lesley knows better than that."

"I didn't know he was a real person."

They explained that John Lesley had mental problems. Nobody knew for sure, but the rumor was that a horse had kicked him in the head.

"Ain't so," Grandpa said.

"That's what pastor told me."

"Don't make it true."

He never worked, had no home, and survived by people taking him in. After a while, he'd leave, and somebody else would put him up and feed him.

"Does he do chores for the people who put him up?" I asked.

"Never seen him do none," she said.

"Have you ever let him stay with you?"

"Couple times," Grandma said. "Nice fella. Ain't got a lick of sense."

I turned to look back at him from the rear window. He was waving to another car.

"So that's John Lesley." Wait'll I tell Kirk and Dennis.

When Grandpa drove those unpaved two-lane country roads, any car behind him would soon catch up. Drivers honked—not out of annoyance, but to say, "How do"—and passed him leaving a cloud of red clay. Grandpa lifted a finger off the steering wheel and nodded to them. "How do?" And hummed right through the dust.

They grew cotton, watermelon, corn, and sugarcane. Dennis and I would take a butcher knife to the sugarcane field, hack a piece off a stalk and, with our teeth, strip off the bamboo-like skin which left a sweet white stick. We chewed the stick, swallowing the juice, and spitting out the pulp.

Dennis and I chased the chickens and the guineas in the

front yard, but they were way too fast and we never caught one. They ran, scared to death, the moment you got near them. One day I set a trap. On the dirt patch where the chickens walked around, I put a stick attached to a string propped up underneath one side of a cardboard box. A hen, with a line of four little fuzzy yellow chicks following behind, paraded by. When she walked underneath the box, I pulled the string. The hen avoided the box as it dropped down, but a little chick was trapped. I carefully lifted the box and grabbed the little feather-ball. The chick was twisting and chirping like mad. Mama hen pivoted and flew directly at my eyes. I dropped the chick. Mom retrieved her, and they scrambled away.

"She almost poked your eye out!" Dennis said. "She was ready to die for her!"

But it was a horse that almost killed me.

Grandpa and I were bringing in his two big plow horses after a full day in the field.

"You stand over yonder," he said, motioning for me to stand off to the side while he removed the horses' harnesses.

To get a better view, I moved over and stood close behind one of the horses. When Grandpa removed the collar from the horse's neck, the horse stood on his front legs and kicked his back legs in the air. The hooves came within an inch of my face.

"Boy, what you doin'?!" Grandpa screamed. "I told you to stand yonder! That horse almos' knocked you dead!"

"I wanted to see what you were doing."

"Don't you know enuff not to git behind a horse when you set it free? They kick so fast you cain't git out of the way."

"Sorry, Grandpa, I didn't know that."

"Oh, foot. John Lesley knows better 'n that."

Grandpa took stalks of sugarcane to a nearby farm. There was a large round wooden hub on the ground, and attached to the hub was a long pole parallel to the ground about four feet high. The pole was tied to a mule that walked round and round the hub. Grandpa fed the sugar cane stalks into an opening in the hub, which slowly swallowed up cane and ground it. The juice flowed into a huge, steaming vat, its fire stoked from the gigantic woodpile stacked off to one side. Finally, there was a metal chute, a little narrower than the ramp on a kid's slide in the park. Down the chute flowed a thick brown goo—molasses, or 'lasses as Grandpa called it.

In the mornings, even before Grandma made breakfast, we'd pretend we had to go to the outhouse and head over to the huge watermelon patch. We'd select one that looked ripe, bust it open by dropping it, and dive face down into it. The chickens fought each other for the seeds we shot out. Grandma wondered why we didn't eat more breakfast.

"After ah done made biscuits an' fat back? You boys better eat 'cuz ain't goin' be nothin' 'til later."

Grandpa was also the country barber. He charged 25 cents a head, and after farming all day, he cut hair for hours. I think he loved having a stage to tell jokes more than he wanted the money.

"He was a good barber, too, Dad. Better than you."

Dad laughed.

Every day, all summer, whenever the mood struck us, we ran down to the sugarcane field or to the watermelon patch and chewed and ate until our jaws got tired. It didn't seem legal.

They grew berries and vegetables. They used the two plow horses in the summer to round up the grain that was stored to feed the livestock.

From a window, I watched Grandpa, Grandma, and some men they hired load hay with pitchforks and stack the bales in the barn to feed the horses all year. It looked so fun, I asked Grandma if I could help.

"You too liddle. You ain't nothin' be a tetch. It's too hot. Cain't handle it."

I begged her every day until she relented.

"Now if it gits too much, you say somthin' ya heah."

"Yes, ma'am."

"I'm gonna be watchin' you."

"Yes, ma'am. But I'll be fine."

The pitchfork looked a lot lighter from the front porch. So did the hay. After fifteen minutes, each scoop weighed five pounds more than the last one. I wilted in the heat, got dizzy, and passed out.

"I ain't gonna say I tried to tell ya'," she said when I woke up. "Tain't as easy as it looks."

On television, barns don't smell funny. In real life, they reek. Grandpa and I carried buckets of "slop"—leftover food mixed with corn, watermelon rinds, and potato peels—to feed the hogs he kept in the barn. I held my breath, dumped the stuff into the trough, and ran out.

"Whatcha hurry?" he said. "Pigs ain't goin' nowhere."

Grandma was short and sturdy and all business. I tried to imagine her forty years younger—and I could see my mother in her face.

One morning after a rainfall, Grandma and I were walking in the field to feed the mules. We came to a four-inch bed of water.

"Uh-oh. There go my tennis shoes."

"Git on my back," she said.

"Get on your back?"

"Git on my back an' I'll tote you across." She pointed at her rubber boots.

"I can't do that, Grandma."

"You ain't heavy. Git on my back, an' I'll tote you across."

I hopped on her back. She toted me across the waterbed as

if I was no heavier than a ladybug.

"Let's feed the mules. Then I'll tote you back."

All the country boys walked barefoot. No trail was too rocky. The first time I tried to do the same, my feet bled. The country kids laughed at the "city sissies." No matter how much we tried, we could not walk around out there without tennis shoes, or sandals at the very least.

I became friends with a boy my age named Charles. We did everything together. We swam in my grandparents' creek, where Charles grabbed a tree vine like Tarzan and swung way out and over before plunking down into the water. It took a while, but I worked up the nerve to do it, too. We sat in truck-tire inner-tubes and floated on the water. We bathed in the creek using the Ivory soap bars Grandpa said to take with us.

"They float. Won't lose 'em."

Charles and I walked to a little store run by a humorless white man who leaned against the wall the whole time we were in there, moving only to collect the money.

"Whatcha want, boy?" he said when we walked in. "Ah said, whatcha want, boy?"

I had never seen a customer treated like that.

"Potato," Charles said.

"What kind of potato, boy? Osh potato?"

"Yes, sir, osh potato."

"Then why didn't ya say so? Cain't read yo' mind, now can I?"

"No, sir."

"Well, all right then."

I couldn't take anymore.

"Look, mister, why—"

Charles grabbed my arm and shook his head. He also asked for an RC Cola and a Moon Pie and we left.

"You let him speak to you like that?"

"Like what?" Charles said.

"Like you were a piece of shit."

"It's different down here," he said.

It sure was. On the train, we passed through small town depots with two arrows painted on the walls pointing to rest-rooms. One arrow would point to a door with a sign over it: "Colored Only."

The year before, Mom and Dad had taken us to the Century drive-in to see *To Kill a Mockingbird*. I asked so many questions that they told me to shut up so they could watch the movie. But this was real. And it was really like that movie.

Grandpa, several times a week, picked tomatoes and berries from the garden, then went to the field to tear off several ears of corn. He put them in a box, set it in the car, came back hours later, and sat at the kitchen table, humming as he counted the coins from his pocket.

"Grandpa, where did you go?"

"To town to sell my produce."

"Can I go with you?"

"Next time. Just don't git in my way."

When we got to town, he drove down a street lined with tidy houses. We got out and rang the first doorbell.

"'Mornin' ma'am, y'all need anythin'?" Grandpa said holding his box.

The lady said, "No, boy, and I thought I told you that two days ago." She picked through the box. "You have anything fresh?"

He assured her that he had picked everything that morning.

"How much for this?" She picked up an ear of corn and fingered it.

"Ten cents."

"Ten cents for this? It ain't even near ready. I'll take two for ten cents."

"Yes, ma'am."

We got back in the car and drove to the next house.

Most people were rude, and almost all called him "boy" even though he was ten to thirty years older than the white housewives haggling with him. He may have made three or four dollars that morning.

"Why does he put up with it?" I asked Mom when Grandpa and I got back. "He doesn't need the money."

She sighed. "No, he doesn't. Grandma even told him to 'quit that foolishness.' But Grandpa feels funny about money. He's always afraid he's going to run out."

"Run out? He's got everything he needs."

"That's the way he is, always has been. We just let him alone. You should, too."

"Well, I'm not going anymore."

Then there was church—the hot, wooden country church with the big, earthy country preacher.

Dad shook his head. "All that hollerin' and whoopin'. I couldn't stand it. I like to be talked to like I'm an adult. I don't like to be preached at."

Grandpa's wooden church had a heavy preacher who pounded the Bible and wiped his face with a white handkerchief that he stuffed in his breast pocket and then whipped out again for another wipe.

People in the pews cooled their faces with paper fans attached to ice cream sticks. On the fans, the local funeral home advertised "traditional family services since 1910."

"Gawd," the preacher shouted, "Gawd says you . . . will . . . find . . . a way!"

The quiet man sitting next to me erupted. "Yes, sah! You will find a way!"

Then the man behind me stood, "Tell it, Rev! Tell it!"

I wondered whether I was being rude by not saying anything. I'd never seen anything like it. In L.A., we went to a polite church with low-key sermons delivered by a guy who looked like an accounting clerk.

Here people got up. They waved. They jumped up and screamed. Some fell to their knees. Everybody was "brotha" and "sista." A man cried. A woman passed out.

Dad shook his head. "Couldn't take all that 'testifyin'.' But I'll give 'em this. They got good singin'."

The choir had at least three singers with voices as beautiful and powerful as that of Aretha Franklin. When I said this to Grandpa on the way home, I expected him to ask who she was.

"You mean the Reverend Franklin's daughter?" he said.

"Who?"

"Boy, you don't know Rev Franklin?"

"Sueberta," he turned to his wife, "boy don't know Rev Franklin."

"Lawdy!" Grandma said.

Reverend C. L. Franklin, I learned, besides being a fine gospel singer, was the most popular and respected preacher in the South, far more well-known than the "Queen of Soul."

Dad said he wished he'd gotten to know Grandpa and Grandma. He met them only once shortly after he and Mom married.

"You know," I said, "I was sitting in the tub, and I heard Mom in the next room complaining about you to Grandma and Grandpa."

"Uh-oh."

"When she left the room, Grandma said, 'You know, I do believe she's too hard on that boy.'"

"Uh-huh," Grandpa said, "'tain't nothin' wrong with that boy."

"They said that?" Dad said. "Well, I'll say."

The summers down on the farm were glorious.

Mom was born and raised on this magnificent land, where her big, rowdy family grew or raised everything they needed. They were self-sufficient. It was a big deal for a black family to own a farm and theirs was a large one that had been in her family for generations. It made them a kind of Depression-era Bible Belt black gentry, who even managed to send Mom and her youngest brother "away for schoolin'." Mom never knew about a Great Depression. She and her brothers ate well, and made money selling the surplus.

Dad's mother lived in rented rooms, often awakening him in the middle of the night. "Git dressed," she'd say.

They would tip-toe down the steps in the darkness to jump the rent. He had no choice but to walk into little country stores to buy food and put up with demeaning service—assuming the store would even extend service. No wonder Dad couldn't wait to get out of the country, and isn't the least bit nostalgic about the place.

"Me and your mother were in two different worlds down there," Dad said, getting up for another cup. "Night and day."

Dad wanted to hear about the time I stayed with Aunt Juanita.

On the way to Huntsville one summer, we stopped off in Chattanooga, Tennessee. Mom and Dennis stayed with cousins. I spent two weeks with my mother's sister, Aunt Nita, whose husband, Eddie, had introduced my parents.

Aunt Nita, like everybody down here, called my mother Ola.

"Ola, it's so nice see you! Oh, my goodness, your boys are so skinny. And I thought they'd be fattened up by now. Does your Momma ever feed you?"

"Just bread and water."

"Larry," Mom said. "Stop it."

Their orderly little house sat down the street from Black Draught, a laxative factory. They bought the house right after they married, and stayed there for going on twenty years. Aunt Nita's friends had long ago moved into bigger houses in better neighborhoods. But Uncle Eddie was having none of it. The house, like his car and his barbershop, was "bought and paid for."

They were sisters, all right. Aunt Nita's face resembled Mom's. And they were both light-skinned with soft hair. Aunt Nita barely finished the seventh grade, and bragged about her husband who "darned near finished high school." She felt lucky to be married, and even luckier that someone as learned and worldly as Uncle Eddie had married her.

"Child, you should hear him talkin' those politics."

Aunt Nita was heavy, but never fretted about her weight. She liked to eat and considered a round, well-fed husband a patriotic duty. She liked big "church hats" and pinned them with fresh flowers. She wore dresses and heels, even while cooking and cleaning. Her house was spotless. She even color-coordinated the little squares of soap placed in glass bowls on either side of the sink in the perfumed bathroom.

Glass was everywhere. The kitchen tabletop was glass. You could have looked through it and seen the floor had Aunt Nita not covered every square inch of the tabletop with homemade place mats. That glass tabletop wouldn't have lasted very long in our house before somebody slammed something down and broke it. But no one slammed anything in this house. No one shouted. No one even raised a voice. They practically whispered.

Why wouldn't Dad, as a single man looking for a good wife, want to meet Juanita's sister?

When Uncle Eddie got up in the morning, his bed was already made up, hotel neat, before his second cup of coffee.

Each night, Aunt Nita laid out his clothes for the next day. She allowed him to select the ties, but she retained the right to overrule.

"Tomorrow, I think your blue suit. It just came back from the cleaners. And that spot finally came out. Had to send it back two times."

"Whatever you say, Honey."

Aunt Nita and her three hundred pounds sprinted to the door when Uncle Eddie pulled in the driveway. Once inside, he stood in the bedroom and removed his suit coat, tie bar, tie, cuff links, white shirt, belt, pants, and dress shoes. He handed them to Aunt Nita in exchange for his robe that she held open for his arms to slide though.

She brought his slippers, pipe, and the *Chattanooga Times*, and he settled into the easy chair and waited for dinner.

"How did it go today?" she asked.

He talked about the barbershop and the customers. She listened to his complaints and made suggestions.

"Well, the last time you gave him credit, it took him two months to pay. Don't cut his hair so short next time. Then he'll have to come back sooner. If he don't, he'll look like a gangster."

Uncle Eddie vented about the latest outrage committed by the Democrats. She asked about his stocks.

"Up an eighth of a point, might even split two-for-one."

She didn't have a clue what that meant.

"Oh, that's wonderful, Honey."

Uncle Eddie complained about the economy and how the Democrats "foul it up."

"Well, I know you goin' to do somethin' about it."

She winked at me.

"Dinner is 'bout ready. Come to the table in two minutes. Wash your hands."

"Ain't you going downtown tomorrow?" Uncle Eddie asked.

"No, Honey. Friday."

"Well, take the money you need from my wallet. If it ain't enough, let me know."

"All right, Honey."

They had already said more to each other than Mom and Dad did in a month.

Dinner was five courses, followed by an after-dinner shot of whiskey.

"How did you like the soup tonight? Wasn't too hot?"

"No, Sweetie, it was perfect."

If he had asked for toothpick, she would have grabbed an ax and chopped down a tree to make sure he got a fresh one. She again brought him a pipe and tobacco, sat next to him, and watched whatever he wanted on television.

"Honey, I'm thinking about having a few of the men from the caucus over next Saturday. Would that be too much trouble?"

It was like asking the dog if he wanted to go out for a w.a.l.k.

"You mean I get to use my new silverware?" she said excitedly.

Aunt Nita planned for Saturday like D-Day. The house was small so that every bit of space had to be used efficiently. How many people? Where would they sit?

What would she serve? What did she serve last time?

Her stuffed turkey was a hit last month, but she'd sooner use a box of "store bought" cake mix before she served the same thing twice. When to serve it? Last time there had been a minor crisis. Eddie's caucus hadn't quite finished strategizing the fall election when she brought out the salads.

"Too early. That ain't gonna happen again. But it ain't my fault they so darn long-winded."

She took pride in doing everything by herself—no assistant, no helper, no servers, and no one to help clean up afterward. She made the desserts from scratch. This time there would be three homemade peach cobblers, two cherry pies, three sweet potatoes pies, and two cakes—one angel food and one devil's food.

Cooking started Thursday.

"Now you just stay out of the way."

"Can I at least help set the table?" I asked Saturday morning.

She allowed me to set out the knifes, forks, appetizer forks, spoons, soup spoons, dessert spoons, and the cloth napkins and holders.

"No, no, no, boy, that spoon there. Don't tell me y'all don't know how to set a proper table?"

"No, Aunt Nita. We don't use dessert spoons."

"Oh, my goodness! Bet Ola has to hide your sorry behind when she throws a party."

When I told her that we never had a party, Aunt Nita practically had to be resuscitated.

"No party? What does she do when Randy has folks over for dinner?"

"Dad doesn't bring anybody over for dinner."

She needed smelling salts.

"Ola ain't never cooked nothin' for your father's folks?"

"No."

"Oh, my Lord, my goodness, my goodness. I'm gonna have to talk to that girl."

Saturday was a big success.

After dinner and when the compliments were over, the women fanned out to the living room, and the men to the front porch which had been screened in to protect against the Tennessee flying bugs.

The women laughed and hooted about church and their children and other people. The men discussed politics. When the political talk ran dry, they sat and smoked pipes, the quiet broken only by the laughter of the wives inside.

After the party, Uncle Eddie went to bed and I helped Aunt Nita with the dishes.

"Ola ain't never had a party. Well, I'll say. I'm gonna have to talk to that girl."

"Dad, before you met Mom, how many times had they had you over for dinner?"

"Bunch of times," he said. "And I thought, damn, and she has a sister?"

"Bet you thought Mom would drop rose petals when you got up to take a leak."

"Well," he said, "not every time."

He didn't know that I met his mother on one trip. I only saw her once.

"I want to meet Dad's mother," I told Mom during one of the summers we spent with Aunt Nita and Uncle Eddie in Chattanooga.

"I met her before," Uncle Eddie said. "Nice lady. Ain't got no phone."

Uncle Eddie had her neighbor's phone number who then contacted her. Uncle Eddie drove Aunt Nita, Mom, and me three hours to Athens.

The wallpaper was peeling in the living room of the small house. The room had a big lumpy couch with a Folger's coffee can holding up one end. A small television set was in the corner on top of a TV tray table. The television was on, the sound was down, the screen flickering. On a small table in the opposite corner sat an old desk fan with the blades spinning.

"Hot down he-ah, ain't it?" she said.

There was a black bug crawling up the wall behind Dad's mother. She followed my eyes to it, took a look, turned back, and gave it no thought.

"How's Ran treatin' you, Honey?" she asked Mom.

She was tiny and short with an apron around her waist. Her flabby little arms waved off flies.

"How's yo daddy?"

"Fine, thank you," I said. I didn't know what to call her. Grandma? Mrs. Elder?

"You know he writes me nearly every month." She pushed up her glasses and waved off a fly. "Yep, pert near every month." She went to the bedroom and came out with a stack of envelopes. "A boy down yonder comes an' reads it to me. Pert near every month."

"Yes, ma'am," I said.

Uncle Eddie, Aunt Nita, and Mom talked about the summer heat. Dad's mother kept staring at me. How did she survive? There was no car anywhere around. Did people bring her food? What does she do all day? What was she doing when we pulled up? Even the television had bad reception. No phone? The nearest neighbor was too far for her to walk to. What did Dad do down here when he was my age? What did he do when he came home from school? What did he play with? There were no kids around. It was the first time I was glad I had brothers—even Dennis.

"You has yo' daddy's eyes," she said.

"Yes, ma'am."

Aunt Nita talked about the next rainfall and how long the one last month lasted. Dad's mom continued staring.

She thanked my aunt and uncle for bringing me and said it was nice seeing Ola again.

"You the only grandbaby I ever met," she said.

"Yes, ma'am."

She kissed me on the cheek and hugged me hard.

"Nex' time I wan'cha to spend a night or two, stay with me a spell," she said. "Would you like that?"

"Yes, ma'am."

"Boy," Aunt Nita asked me, "ain't there anythin' you want to ask yo' grandmama? What you said in the car. Go 'head."

There was so much I planned to ask her. My dad's father? Where was he? Tell me about him? Why did you have only one child?

She seemed so tired, so sad. I just wanted to leave.

"What was my father like?" I asked.

"Well," she said, "I tell you. Dat boy worked hard. Dat's the one thing 'bout him. He worked hard."

Two gray cats wandered around.

"I have a cat," I said.

"I like cats," she said.

"Yes ma'am. So do I."

I asked if I could take a picture of her.

"Yes, go out yonder. Right 'der is fine." She patted her hair and pushed up her glasses.

I took a picture of her standing on the porch. She didn't smile. She didn't wave, just stood—arms to the side, looking straight ahead. We stayed about two hours, then drove back to Chattanooga.

"Well, that's your daddy's mama," Mom said.

"That sounds like her," Dad said when I finished the story. "Ain't much for small talk. That's my momma. Did the best she could."

It was 9:15.

20

"NOBODY FUCKS WITH MY FAMILY"

"You weren't like your brother. You gave us almost no trouble."

"No, I just never got caught."

Dad laughed.

"No, I'm serious, there was a lot of stuff going on that you didn't know about."

"Like what?" he asked.

"Oh, some not so major, some major."

"Like what?"

"Remember the red apartments up at the corner?" I said. "You told us to stay away from them because of the kind of people who rented them."

"Yeah, weren't there some shootin's or wife beatin's or somethin' over there?"

"Yes, that's why you told us to stay away."

There was a man who lived there by himself. He'd drink and stumble around outside and yell at us when we played baseball in the street. We'd gather around him and taunt him, which only made him angrier.

"You kids!" he screamed. "You damn kids! Ju—just le—leave me a—alone."

We'd pretend to throw things at him. He'd flinch and we'd laugh some more.

Dad shook his head. "Larry, that's just cruel."

"I didn't say I was proud of it, Dad. I'm just telling you I wasn't a choir boy."

One day I said to Dennis, "Let's get that guy."

"You know what Mom and Dad said."

"Ah, c'mon. No one's going to find out."

We got a couple of peashooters, looked around, crept up to his door, and aimed the peashooters. Bap! Bap! Bap! We blew the hard little brown peas out of the straw-like shooters at his front door. We shot so many and so hard that from the inside, it must have sounded like machine gun fire. But even after shooting, reloading, and shooting again several times, he didn't come out. He had probably fallen asleep so drunk that he didn't hear the noise, or was in no condition to get up and do anything about it. We ran home.

About a half-hour later, the doorbell rang. I looked through the peephole and went numb.

"Who is it?" Mom yelled from the kitchen.

"Nobody," I said.

The bell rang again. "Who is it?"

"Nobody."

It rang again. "What's the matter with you? I'll get it myself." Mom opened the door and there stood the man from the red apartments. He was not happy.

"Yur boys," he said, steadying himself against the screen door. "Yur boys had these, these, I dunno whatcha call 'em—bean shooters and they went psssst, psssst."

"They did what?"

"You know." Putting his hand to his mouth to demonstrate, he held up an imaginary peashooter and blew through his thumb and index finger.

"Psssst, psssst. And my door went ping! ping! ping! And ah wuz tryin' to sleep. But they kep' on with that ping! ping! ping!"

He accurately described what we'd done, how we did it, and precisely the number of times we'd blasted his door.

Mom nodded, growing angrier by the second. "Yes. Okay. I understand. . . . Absolutely. . . . I certainly will take care of it. And you can be sure of that. . . . Yes, you're right. No excuse for it. None. . . . Yes, they're right here. . . . Yes, I guarantee you they will be punished. Their father will be home soon, and he'll see to it."

We were in for a hellacious whipping. Dad and Mom had told us to stay away from those apartments, and especially to leave that "crazy alcoholic" alone. This was a "wait for your father to come home" time if there was ever one. And this time, the punishment would probably fit the crime. I prayed for divine intervention, but I also made plans for my afterlife.

"Tha—than—thanksss. I 'preciate it if ya do sumptin' 'bout it right 'way, right 'way. Tha—than—thanksss." The man from the red apartments turned and staggered back down the stairs.

Mom slammed the door, walked back to the kitchen, and shook her head. "Drunk-ass liar. Are you two ready to eat?"

Dad laughed. "You were the ringleader."

"Yup."

"You sure as hell dodged one that time. If there's anythin' your mother hates, it's a drunk."

We were the second black family to move onto Haas Avenue. Soon there were more. And there was a lot of friction between the growing number of black kids and the dwindling number of white kids. My second-grade class had a "paper drive." The teacher asked students to go door to door and collect old papers. I don't remember what the school did with all the bundles of papers, but I assumed it had to do with recycling.

Dennis and I went together, and he pulled the wagon that we used to stack the papers. The homeowners, usually housewives, were friendly and warm, quite happy to rid themselves of old newspapers they'd accumulated over several days.

"Hello," I said. "I go to 74th Street School, and we're asking for old newspapers for our paper drive."

"Certainly, young man. Step around to the back."

Dennis and I would often walk around the "For Sale" sign, and head to the garage where we loaded the papers onto the wagon.

"Thank you," we said.

"Anytime."

Every other house seemed to have a "For Sale" sign on the front lawn. And I didn't know why.

"Mom, people around here sure move a lot," I said, after my first day of door-to-door.

"Yes, they do."

"Are we going to move again, too?"

"I don't think so," she said. "Not for a while."

My new elementary school was changing from a majority white student body to a majority black one. The school population took longer to "convert" than the neighborhood. Even after the white families moved away—and they did in waves—they still drove the kids to 74th Street School until sixth-grade graduation. I never had a black teacher until the seventh grade, although I later found out that my fifth-grade teacher, Mrs. Dunne, was actually an extremely light-skinned woman whom I falsely assumed was white.

At my first elementary school, the one near the old house on

Valencia, I once had a black substitute teacher. I had never seen a black teacher, and I was riveted. She was pretty, forceful, and totally in charge. Usually substitute teachers seemed nervous in front of a class that was used to their regular teacher. And the kids knew that a sub teacher would be there for only one day, so the class tried her patience by "acting out." What is a one-day sub teacher going to do to you? But this teacher didn't take any crap. The first time a kid spoke without being asked, she sent him down to the principal's office.

"Who's next?" she said. There was no more trouble after that. She was, I guess, an early "role model."

Dad shook his head. "I never had a white teacher."

I made friends with the kids in the other families just moving in. My closest friend, David, lived one house away on the same side of the street. Dietrich, another friend, lived one block up. He was a likeable, slightly overweight kid who always wore shiny black Spanish boots, rather than tennis shoes like the rest of us.

One day, when we were in high school, I needed to go to the public library on Crenshaw Boulevard for a homework assignment. David and Dietrich wanted to play basketball.

"Naw, I gotta go to the library."

"All right, fuck it," David said. "We'll go with you."

David was half a grade behind me, but way ahead of the curve in his coolness quotient. His father was black and his mother Japanese. When David's father was in the military, he was stationed in Japan where he met David's mother. David was "fine," according to the girls in school, and he smoked cigarettes, drank beer, and occasionally smoked dope. He had grown a big, round, fluffy Afro—well before the rest of us could overcome our parents' objections to 'fros.

As we walked down Crenshaw, two white kids around our age were walking toward us.

"Got a cigarette?" David asked them.

The taller one reached into his shirt pocket and pulled out a pack of Marlboros. He opened the top and held it out. David reached for a cigarette, but the guy closed the box and pulled it away.

"No, man," he said, "I was just showing you I only got two left. Sorry."

"Aw, c'mon," David said. "Gimme one."

"Sorry. Only got two left." They walked away.

"Fuck you, then!" David shouted, and thrust his right fist in the air. "Black power!"

The whites guys stopped, said something to each other, likely deciding whether to do something about this disrespect. They decided against it and kept walking.

"Leave it alone," I said.

"Yeah," Dietrich said, "the dude only had two left. Let it slide."

"Black power!" David shouted again.

At the library, I found what I needed and sat down. David and Dietrich picked out something to read. A half-hour later, the white guy, the tall one with the cigarettes, tapped David hard on the shoulder.

"You still got something to say?"

Startled, but defiant, David said, "Damn right!"

"Okay, then step outside."

"You got it."

David got up, followed the guy, and then turned around to see that neither Dietrich nor I had budged. "David's mouth got him here," Dietrich and I thought, "let him talk his way out of it."

"What? You guys aren't coming? You're just going to leave me hangin'? Aw, c'mon!"

"Let's go," I said.

It was like a Hell's Angel convention outside. At least twenty white guys, some sitting on motorcycles, waited for us.

"Now, motherfucker," the white kid said, "what was all this shit?" He put his fist in the air.

Shaking, David said, "Aw, man, it was just, you know, a black power salute."

"Fuck black power, motherfucker, white power!"

"Yeah," David said, "well, you know, that's cool, too."

Several guys got off their bikes and headed toward us.

"Look," I said, "This is stupid. It was just a misunderstanding. He wanted a cigarette and we thought this dude was giving him one, that's all. No point in fighting over something like this."

No one said anything to us. They mumbled to each other for about a minute. Some stared at us and revved their motorcycles.

"Forget it. Let's go," said one of them. "Get on my bike and let's get out of here." The kid with the cigarette hopped on his seat and raised his fist.

"You got lucky this time, motherfucker."

Dad shook his head. "You could have been killed. What I'd tell you about writin' a check your ass can't cash?"

"Well, there's more. Remember we were talking about my friend Perry?"

Months later, Perry and I saw the cigarette kid walk down the street and into a house. I told Perry about the library.

"Let's fuck him up," Perry said.

That night, I got Mom's car, and Perry picked up a cinderblock. We cut off the headlights. Perry got out and threw the cinderblock through the kid's big picture window. Smash! We drove away, waited about a half hour, and drove back. Two squad cars with flashing lights were there and police officers were talking to his parents and taking notes. Perry and I laughed. The kid's family moved a few months later.

"That don't make no sense for you to pull somethin' like that.

And you wonder why those folks moved away after we moved in."

I admitted it was wrong and stupid, but I wanted him to know I wasn't any angel—far from it.

"Well, at least you guys never shot anybody."

"Funny you should say that."

"Uh-oh."

There was the matter of Douglas.

He was big, tall, and muscular, and dressed better than anyone—a "player," with a demonic little moustache. Where he got the money nobody knew because he didn't have a job, but Douglas always drove sports cars. He'd drive a Triumph for a while, the car would break down, and he'd scrape together the money to fix it. Later, he'd suddenly show up in a Spyder. It would break down, and he'd fix it and trade it in for a Jensen-Healy. They were used, but when he rumbled up the street—nice and slow so everybody could look—he turned heads.

"What an asshole," we all thought.

He lived several blocks away, but dated a girl on my street so he was always near.

He was always pushing me around. Dennis even noticed.

"You better do something to get that motherfucker off your back," he said.

Then, during gym class, Douglas turned the shower water to cold, cupped his hands around the showerhead, and directed a stream of ice-cold water on my back. Douglas and the other kids laughed, and he dared me to do anything about it. I didn't.

I played gin rummy, and was good at it. A bunch of guys in the neighborhood got up a game, and I was winning. Douglas kept losing, and would double down each time. Each time he lost.

"You owe me eighteen dollars, Douglas," I said.

"I'm good for it." He promised to pay the next day.

But the next day he put me off. Then again, and again. So I

went to Bruce, a tough guy in the neighborhood, and told him that Douglas refused to pay.

"If you get my money, I'll give you ten percent."

"Bet on it," Bruce said. "I'll get your money from that motherfucker."

I went to Douglas's house.

"Bruce said he was going to kick your ass if you don't pay me my money."

"Oh, really. Meet me at Bruce's house," he said.

"All right." I couldn't wait for Bruce to beat the shit out of him. It was worth not getting my eighteen bucks to see that.

He drove to Bruce's house and knocked on the door.

"Larry said you going to kick my ass. All right, do it. Let's get it on."

"Oh, man," Bruce said. "Naw, I was just bullshitting. Me and you's cool."

"No, motherfucker," Douglas said. "If you said you're going to kick my ass, let me see you do it."

Bruce completely backed down and denied ever promising to collect my money.

"I don't know where Larry got that shit from," Bruce said.

Douglas then turned to me.

"Now, motherfucker. You ain't never getting your money."

I was completely humiliated.

Everybody knew he owed me the money, and now everybody knew he was never going to pay. My reputation as something less than a tough guy slid even lower. And once you get a reputation as a poot-butt, more abuse and ridicule will surely follow.

I had to do something.

A few days later, while driving Mom's car, I passed Douglas's latest sports car, a blue Triumph, parked in front of a house nowhere near his or his girlfriend's house. The car had broken down and Douglas was nowhere to be seen.

I waited until night and rounded up a few kids from the neighborhood, including Dietrich from the cigarette incident. They all hated Douglas. We got green paint, tomatoes, and eggs. I shut off the headlights, and after making sure that nobody was watching, our three-man posse got out and destroyed his car. We splattered paint all over it and pelted it with eggs and tomatoes.

"I think that's at least eighteen dollars worth of damage," I said to the guys as we slapped hands and laughed.

The next day, Douglas rang the doorbell.

"You fucked up my car," he said.

I denied it.

"Yes you did. I know you did. One of the neighbors saw you. I have a witness."

He was bluffing. I decided to pull a Douglas.

"Really? Then let's go. Let's go and see your witness. I didn't do it. You got somebody who says I did, let's go see him."

He backed down a little, still not quite certain I had done it. I had been adamant. And as long as nobody in my posse broke confidence, I knew I would get away with it. Well, he threatened Ernie, one of the guys with me that night. Douglas told him he knew Ernie was involved because someone else ratted. It was a good bluff, and it scared Ernie into admitting that Dietrich and I had trashed the car.

The next day, Dietrich and I were walking down the street, coming back from the store. We had grocery bags in each hand. Douglas pulled up in another sports car, jumped out, ran over, and hit Dietrich in the face, knocking him down hard. He pulled out a knife-shaped block of wood—something he made in wood shop at school—and waved it at me. I ran around a parked car. He thought that Dietrich and I might rush him, but we were too scared.

"C'mon motherfuckers. I know you fucked up my car. Ernie told me. And I'm gonna get you. I'm gonna kill both of you motherfuckers! Just wait." He got back in his car and drove off. "Just wait, motherfuckers! You guys are dead."

Now I really had to do something. I called Steve, my comic-book friend, who had grown to over six feet tall and hated Douglas as much as the rest of us. He called some of his friends, and I called some more of mine. I went to Douglas's house, threatened him, and told him to meet me on our street the next day after school.

At about 4 p.m. the next day, Douglas led a caravan of eight cars, with some big, mean-looking guy behind each wheel. I only recognized a couple of his guys. Where the rest came from, I had no idea. Slowly, deliberately, they got out of their cars.

But I had my crew, too. I had about ten guys, with sticks, billy clubs, and brass knuckles. We were on one side of the street, and Douglas's guys on the other. No one moved, we just stared and showed our sticks, clubs and fists. On Douglas's side, though, at least two or three had knives. We waited and stared. Somebody had to make the first move.

Suddenly, Dennis came rushing up the street. He was screaming and waving his arms. "Goddamn you, Douglas! You motherfucker! I'm tired of you fucking with my family!"

Dennis stood at the end of my line of guys. He reached into his pocket and pulled out a gun. He aimed it at Douglas.

"This is the last time, you motherfucker!" Dennis was so angry he was shaking. I'd seen him that way many times. "Nobody fucks with my family."

I didn't know what to do. I wanted to scream at Dennis, "What the fuck are you doing?" But a small part of me wanted Dennis to shoot the son-of-a-bitch, or at least wing him. I just froze.

Douglas didn't move. He said nothing. He stared back at Dennis, almost daring him to pull the trigger. Dennis shot the gun. A whiff of dirt flew up at Douglas's feet.

A black-and-white police cruiser appeared at the bottom of our hill, racing toward us. Dennis threw the gun in a bush behind me. We all stuffed our weapons in our pants, tossed them inside the cars, or threw them in the bushes—and hoped the cops didn't do a search.

"What's going on here?" one officer said.

"Nothing," we said.

"Nothing?" said the officer. "I got a call that something was going down. Bunch of cars. Bunch of guys. And nothing?"

"Somebody was wrong," we said. "Just a discussion."

The cops said something to each other.

"All right. Don't make us come back. If we do, everybody's going to jail."

They drove away.

We lingered for a while, then broke up, and everybody went home. Nothing else happened. Everybody just decided to forget about the whole thing.

"But," I told Dad, "I never got my eighteen dollars."

Dad shook his head. "That was really stupid. Did Dennis miss on purpose or was his aim just way off?"

"I asked Dennis that. And you know him. He'd say one thing one time, then another thing another time. I don't know. The two sides were standing close, right across the street. So it was practically point-blank. But Dennis was shaking, the way he gets when he's really mad. So I don't know."

"Where did he get the gun?"

"I found out that he got it from a guy in the neighborhood. It was a .22 and I don't know what happened to it. Dennis wouldn't say, and I didn't want to know."

"The shit you pulled, Larry." Dad buried his head in his hands. "My God, why didn't you stop Dennis—at least tell him to put the gun down? Somebody could have gotten killed. And your brother could have been sent to prison for murder. All 'cuz someone owed you eighteen dollars."

"Yeah," I said. "Not smart."

"You got that right." He kept shaking his head. "Well, you're right. You sure got away with a lot of crap I didn't know about."

· 21 ·

"YOU WEREN'T LIKE YOUR BROTHER"

Even with all the shit I pulled, Dad was right. I wasn't like my little brother. He came out of the womb pissed.

"What's the matter?" Mom said, when I came home from a high school party one night. She could tell I was upset.

"Nothing," I said.

"You mean you don't want to tell me."

"I mean you don't want to hear it."

"Try me."

I told her Dennis and I had walked to a house party given by friends who lived one block over.

"Larry, your brother is in the back smoking marijuana," somebody said. And there was Dennis sitting on a beanbag chair just toking away.

"Marijuana!" Mom was hysterical.

"So I said 'Dennis, Let's go home.' He stood up, went like this," I imitated him inhaling, "and he blew the smoke right in my face."

"I'll talk to him."

Then she launched into another one of her why-can't-you-

and-Dennis-get-along pleas.

"Some day, I don't know when," I said, "Dennis is going to kill or be killed."

She was outraged.

"It's not a wish, Mom. It's a prediction."

While we were all scared of Dad, Dennis was the most afraid. His feelings were hurt easily, and he masked it by joking and showing off, being defiant at school and at Sunday school. I brought home A's. He brought C's, D's and, increasingly, F's.

Dad poured another cup of coffee. Talking about Dennis unsettled him.

"I wish I had known. I wish I had known." Dad put his head in his hand. "I could have done somethin' about Den. I know I could."

When we were kids, I'd tease Dennis, and he'd throw his plastic model plane—the one he'd spent hours gluing together—at me so hard that it shattered when I ducked and it hit the wall. We argued once during breakfast, and he picked up his plate—that had just been stacked with fresh pancakes and butter and syrup—and threw it at me. He missed, but splattered the uneaten breakfast on the walls, the curtains, and the floor. Dad, as usual, was not home, and my mother cleaned up the mess and never told him what happened.

Dennis was handsome, funny, and charismatic. But he decided to be the anti-Larry. If I wanted to do something, he refused. If I excelled, he was indifferent or pretended to be.

After I stopped working for Dad, I got a job at the burger and hot dog concession in the basement of the museum off Exposition Boulevard. I was a good worker, and they asked me to recommend others who might want to work there. I told Mom, and she told me to get Dennis a job. I didn't want to because I knew we'd end up fighting. We did, and he quit after a few weeks. But even I had to laugh at some of the stuff he would do to amuse himself at this job that bored him to death.

One day, we ran out of Coke for the fountain. It was his job to inform the customers. And they weren't happy. Some had stood in line for over a half hour.

"Sorry, sir, we're out of Cokes."

"Out!?"

"Yes sir, sorry."

After the hundredth time, Dennis decided to shake things up a little.

"Sorry, sir, we're out of Cokes."

"Out?!"

"Yes," Dennis said calmly. "You're familiar with out—opposite of in."

I laughed so hard my stomach hurt.

A studious-looking guy—thick glasses, pocket protector—ordered a couple of burgers, two bags of chips, and a large Coke.

"Sorry, sir, we're out of Coke."

"Out!?" The guy shrieked, waving his hands in consternation.

"Yesss!" Dennis shrieked back, mimicking the gesture. It was hysterical.

I tried to tell him how to do things safely and more efficiently. He deliberately did the opposite of what I told him.

"Dennis, don't hold the hot dog in your hand while pouring on the chili. The chili is hot. You'll get burned."

A man ordered a chili dog. Dennis picked up the hot dog, dipped the scooper, and poured the chili over the dog. It ran over the bun and onto his hand. I could practically smell his skin burning, but he wouldn't let me have the satisfaction of saying, "I told you so." The longer he held that dog, the more his hand burned.

"Oouuuuccchh!" He finally dropped the chili dog on the floor and frantically waved his scalded hand. I enjoyed it. He soon quit.

Dennis graduated from marijuana to barbiturates. Users called them "flatheads." When he took them, he became drunk-like—angry, vicious, and violent. The first time, the high school called my mother—her work phone the only number on file—and asked that she immediately leave work to pick him up. They called him a danger to himself and to others.

He refused to get in her car. She pleaded with him—all this right in front of the main high school entrance.

"Get your hands off me, bitch!" he screamed.

"Please, Dennis, get . . . in . . . the . . . car!"

"You don't tell me what to do! Nobody tells me what to do!"

This went on for some twenty minutes. He finally got in the car and screamed at her all the way home.

"I don't have any freedom!"

"You let Larry and Kirk do things I can't do!"

"I'm a man and you treat me like a child!"

When he got home, he went to his bedroom and slept for ten hours. This scene was re-played over and over. He'd go to school high or get high when he got there. The school would call Mom, she would leave work, then wrestle him into the car while students inside pressed against the windows and watched the show.

She was humiliated. And I had to hear about it from other students. As much as he resented me, Dennis never cursed at Mom when I was there to hear it.

My father never knew. Mom never told him. By the time Dad knew about Dennis's drug use, he was a full-blown addict and a high-school dropout who ran around with guys Mom called "low-lifes and thugs."

"I wish I had known," Dad said repeatedly. "I wish I'd known. I could have done somethin'."

The cold war between Mom and Dad started the day she

quit the restaurant. She didn't want his help in handling the home front—and he wasn't about to volunteer. She got her phone company job and became a supervisor. She showed him! She assumed she was making more money than Dad. She didn't know for sure because he wouldn't say how much he made. They stopped filing their income tax returns jointly so that one side wouldn't know what the other made—even though they stood to save money by filing together.

She vowed not to ask Dad's help for anything, including with Dennis. She considered it a personal failure—and therefore a victory for Dad—if she couldn't deal with Dennis. She wasn't about to give Dad the satisfaction.

Dennis was crying out for help even as his defiance of Mom grew more and more bold. She tried to reason with him and accepted his promises to do better. When he didn't, she made more excuses, and he made more promises.

Dad came home, meanwhile, and went to bed—oblivious to Dennis's demons. Would it have made a difference?

"I don't know," he said. "But I'd have liked to try."

Because Dennis was indifferent to school and drank and did drugs, Mom refused to sign him up for driver's education. Of all the teenagers in the neighborhood, Dennis never learned to drive and was the only one without a license. This enraged him.

One night, he swiped my set of keys for Mom's car. He tried to drive it but crashed the car not even two blocks from the house, ran from the scene, and denied any involvement. Dad came in that night just as Mom was confronting Dennis about the accident. Dad was outraged.

"Did you take those keys?"

Dennis denied it.

"How did that car hit that pole?"

Dennis didn't know.

"So somebody stole your mother's car, crashed it, left the scene, and the neighbors all lied when they said they saw you runnin' away from the crash! Goddammit!" Dad pointed to the cat. "Even Cream Puff is shakin' his head."

Dad stepped over the coffee table, grabbed Dennis, and shook him. He slapped him.

"Don't you lie to me! I'll make you wish you had never lived!"

Dennis broke away and ran from the house. He was gone for several days.

When he came back, he was worse. Things started missing from the house. He would sell them to buy drugs. My collection of record albums disappeared. Ditto for my coin collection.

"No, I haven't seen them," Dennis said when I confronted him.

"Right, I guess Dad stole them."

"Fuck you!"

If he was high, he'd yell at the ceiling about how much he hated me. "God, I hate your guts! I just can't stand that mother-fucker." He'd point to me.

And the feeling was mutual.

Dad said very little. He never knew about the stuff that happened before he got home. He knew Dennis stopped going to school and eventually he learned about the drugs. By then, Dennis came and went when he felt like it and when Dad tried to talk to him, Dennis simply disappeared, sometimes for weeks.

"One day, Dad, I almost killed him. If it weren't for Mom, I would have."

I asked him if he wanted to hear about it. He did.

"Are you sure?"

I promised a friend I'd meet him for breakfast, and had gotten up to shower when I heard it. Dennis was screaming at Mom.

"Fuck you!" "Fuck this!" "Fuck that!"

I lost it. I put on some pants and shoes and ran to the front of the house. I grabbed him by his neck and rammed him against the wall.

"I told you never to talk to her like that! Do you hear me?! Do it again, and I'll kill you!"

He was shaking and scared. I released him. He calmed down and I got into the car and left. About a block away, I realized that I left my wallet with my driver's license. I turned around to get it. I intended to dash right in and out, so instead of pulling in the driveway where the car could be seen from the kitchen—which was where I last left Mom—I just parked on the street.

When I walked in, I heard him again.

"Fuck you!" "Fuck this." "Fuck that."

I charged him.

We fought from the front of the house to the back and to the front again. He broke a dining room chair over me. I threw him into the living room television set. I knocked him down and smashed my fist into his face. He could have hit me with a hatchet—I wouldn't have felt a thing. I kept charging. I pounded him for the years of putting up with his ridicule, for embarrassing Mom by taking pills and fighting with her in front of the whole school, for stealing from me, for endangering Mom and the whole family by bringing his "low-lifes and thugs" into our house, and for all the times he got loaded and—while I was trying to study or play piano—he shouted to anyone who could hear how much he hated me.

I wanted to destroy him.

"Please, Larry, please, you're killing him!"

I wanted to.

She tried to grab my arm as I delivered blow after blow. I shook her away and kept pounding. Dennis had long stopped struggling, and I continued to land blow and after blow.

Mom charged me from behind, jumped on my back, and put her arms around me.

"Please. Please. You're killing him."

"All right. All right," I said.

I stood up over him. He began to stir again.

"Fu—, fu—, f—," he mumbled, weak and battered but still defiant.

I decided to finish the job.

"You want some more! You want some more!"

"Please, Larry, please," Mom cried hysterically. "Just go! Leave! I'll handle this. You . . . just . . . leave."

I left. He never cursed at her again.

Out of all our fights, from the earliest ones over a tricycle, to the ones about him stealing from my piggy bank, to the times he charged me with a butcher knife or with a broken glass bottle, this was where we came the closest to someone getting killed. Dennis was seventeen, and I was eighteen.

Dad came home that night and went to bed, just like any other night.

I wanted out of that house, out of this city, away from Dennis, and away from Dad.

Two weeks later, I was on an airplane bound for college— putting 3,000 miles between Dennis and Dad and me.

That was our last fight.

It wasn't until I took psychology in college that I had a clue about at least one big factor in "what was wrong with Dennis." I read about sibling rivalry. It was as if the author wrote the book after sitting in our home and taking notes.

Because Dennis and I were so close in age, we had many of the same teachers. I made mostly A's. Dennis struggled. Not because he didn't have it. He was quick and sharp. He just didn't care, or pretended not to.

"Why aren't you like your brother?" a teacher would ask. "I don't understand, you brother was always prepared," said another. Or, "This work is poor. Are you sure you're Larry's brother?" Dennis heard this again and again. Today teachers are more sensitive. At least I hope so.

"There's a song," I told Dad, "that goes, 'it must have been cold there in my shadow.' It must have been awful the way teachers and kids compared Dennis to me. To a lot of people, I was a star. My light blinded him."

"Maybe," Dad said, "but that's no excuse. I wish I had known. I could have done somethin'."

But Dad never asked Mom about Dennis, about how he was doing, or what he could do to help. And that's exactly how Mom wanted it. They silently negotiated a policy: Don't ask, don't tell. Would an early intervention by Dad have changed anything?

"You may think so," I told him, "I don't."

"At least I would have liked to try."

"What were you going to do? Beat him? Take away his television set? Make him work at the restaurant? Tell him to do his homework? Put him in drug rehab? He wouldn't go. Mom arranged for counseling. How could you have run the restaurant and baby-sat him at the same time? That would have been a full-time job. He had to make his own mistakes. It's not your fault."

I pointed out to him that Kirk and I had the same parents, the same circumstances, and the same issues. We ate the same food and slept in the same house. We turned out one way, Dennis another. Was Dennis caught in the middle of Mom and Dad's cold war? Was he collateral damage or just a bad seed?

"He cleaned himself up enough to go in the Army. And even the Army couldn't straighten him out. He came out as direction-less as he went in. Dennis was Dennis."

Dad stood up and stretched. He looked at the clock.

"Good, Lord. Need to clean up around here before Sanitation comes by and locks me up."

"Do you need some help?"

"You remember how?"

"Just let me in the back to change. I'll show you, sir, how it's done."

It was 10:30.

It had been eight hours.

But it took a lifetime.

· PART THREE ·

POSTSCRIPT

· 22 ·

DÉTENTE

Hi Son:

It's so wonderful to find after all these years, I have a son that loves and understands me. Thanks. For now I feel like a father for the first time in my life. You are a comfort and strength to me.

You are spoiling me. So what the hell? We love being spoiled by the ones we love.

Dad

Every time we ended a phone call, I told Dad I loved him. He was unnerved a little at first, but I kept doing it. Pretty soon, he said it back, sometimes beating me to it.

"You guys are sickening," Mom said.

Tough lady, my mother.

In 1979, Iranian thugs took Americans hostage and ended up holding them for 444 days. At my Cleveland law firm, young associates gathered in my office—the town hall of the floor—and kicked around possible American responses.

"Diplomacy," offered one.

"Freeze Iranian bank accounts in American banks," said another.

"Encourage other countries in the 'world community' to impose an international trade embargo," suggested another.

"I know what my mother would do," I said.

"What?"

"She'd give them forty-eight hours to set the hostages free. After that, start bombing."

They laughed.

"I'm not kidding," I said. "That's exactly what she would do."

"Oh, come on. Nobody's mother would say that."

"Mine would."

"Oh, please."

"Watch."

I picked up the phone and called her in L.A.

"Mom, what would you do about this hostage thing? Uh-huh. Uh-huh. I see. Okay, Mom. Thanks. Talk later."

"Well, did she say she'd give them forty-eight hours?"

"No, she didn't," I said.

"Hah! Thought so."

"She's mellowing. She said she'd give them seventy-two."

Mom complained about Dad.

"He's in the way when I vacuum." "Stays home all the time." "We can't agree on what to watch on television." "I try to get him to talk, and he won't."

Dad complained about Mom.

"She vacuums when I'm watchin' television." "She doesn't know how loud she talks when she's on the phone." "As soon as I get up, she makes up the bed. I can make up my own bed. She just does it to try and make me not go back to sleep. Sometimes,

I want to go back to sleep."

I umpired.

But after The Talk, Mom said I "switched sides."

"Your father is a poor businessman," Mom said.

"Mom, that's a heavy thing to say about someone who's kept the door open all these years in something as competitive as the restaurant business."

"He hasn't made much money."

"He's paid the house note, the car notes, helped keep the house fixed up, and helped put food on the table. That's a lot. And for a guy who quit school at thirteen, it's pretty impressive."

"You sound like his defense attorney. Is that what you learned when I sent you to law school?"

I considered buying a house in L.A. I brought Mom to take a look.

"It's a great house. You should buy it."

I told her I worried about the debt.

"Sit down."

She told me that our Haas Avenue house was not her choice. She wanted to move into a bigger house in a more upscale neighborhood.

"We could have afforded it. The neighborhood was better. But no-o-o-o, your father wouldn't go for it."

As Mom predicted, the values in the other neighborhood went up at a much faster rate, and now the neighborhood is too pricey for the working class. She and Dad would have had lots of equity, and the mortgage, small by today's terms, would have been long paid off.

"Your father thought small. Don't make the same mistake."

"That's unfair."

"Oh, here you go again. Defending him."

"He's not Donald Trump."

"He was a wimp," she said.

"Wimps don't survive on their own starting at thirteen years old. Wimps don't go back to school in their forties and sit next to teenagers. Thurman wanted to go back to school, but admitted he didn't have the nerve. A wimp doesn't quit his jobs and start a restaurant at forty-seven."

Nothing.

"He wanted to build the restaurant—that's a big dream—and was saving for it. Dad had a small margin of error. What if something went wrong? What if somebody got sick? The money he saved by not buying a bigger house might have been the difference between a restaurant and no restaurant."

Silence.

"And if things had gone a certain way, nothing was stopping you and Dad from moving into a bigger house later."

"Well, we never did."

"Hindsight's 20/20. I'm not saying Dad was right not to reach a little higher, I just want you to try and understand why he didn't."

She stood up. "Let's go."

I put my hands on her shoulders. "Mother, just because my relationship with Dad is better, it doesn't mean ours is any less. It's not two against one."

"Hm-mm. So, are you going to buy this place or not?"

Mom soon figured out how to use my new relationship with Dad to her advantage. She got him to do things he didn't want to do.

"Your father needs a new suit. He won't go shopping."

"Put him on the phone," I said.

"Randolph! Larry. He wants to talk to you."

"Dad, you're going shopping, okay? It's no big deal."

"I really don't feel like goin'."

"Do it for me, Dad. It won't hurt."

He sighed. "All right."

"The sooner you go, the sooner you'll be back. Now give the phone back to Mom. I love you."

"Love you, too."

"Okay, Mom, he's good to go."

"Putting your father on the phone" also worked for things like dental appointments, eye examinations, and regular check-ups. I even got him to take Mom out to a couple of movies.

"You're the only one he listens to," Mom said.

"Your father won't eat," Mom said. "I make him something. He just picks at it."

"Put him on the line. . . . Dad, I'm going to pick you up on Sunday afternoon about 5 o'clock. Wear your blue jacket."

We went to an upscale restaurant.

"Dad, have you ever had crab legs?"

"Does it have bones?"

Before I was born, Dad got a fish bone stuck in his throat. It stayed stuck for several days. He vowed never to eat fish again. Whenever Mom fried fish, she also prepared something separate for him.

"No bones."

He loved the crab legs. Then he ate all of the huge side dishes—the asparagus, the baked potato, an oversized slice of bread—and even bummed me out of one of my crab legs. The man ate like a horse.

I soon discovered the problem.

"Mom cooks just about the same thing every day," he said on

the way home. "Guess it's easier for her. She gets mad if I complain. So I don't say anythin', but I get tired of the same thing."

I told Mom.

"All he has to do is tell me what he wants."

"He's afraid to say anything."

"He's afraid of me?"

"It isn't his appetite, Mom. It's the menu."

"Well, I'll say."

I found out that Dad and Mom watched "Jeopardy" every night, so I decided to come over one evening and watch it with them.

Dad sat in his chair, Mom on the couch, and me in a chair in the middle.

"Who is Will Mays?" I said.

"What is Lake Eerie?" I blurted.

"What is Tibet?!" I exclaimed, triumphantly.

I looked around. I swear, I heard crickets chirping.

"Don't you guys ever shout out the answers?"

They shook their heads, no.

"Why?"

Nothing.

"Why? Sometimes you know the answers, don't you?"

"Sometimes."

"Or you think you might know them, right?"

"Sometimes."

"Then why don't you shout them out?"

Nothing.

"Jesus, that's what makes the thing fun. You see how you do against the contestants and see how you do against each other. You just sit here like stumps?"

Nothing.

I turned off the television.

"I get it. Dad, you don't really know the answers. Not your fault. Mom, I know you know a lot of them."

Nothing.

"Dad, if Mom shouts out answers and gets them right, you'll think she's showing off to make you feel stupid, won't you?"

Nothing.

"I'll take that as a yes."

"Mom, you don't shout them out because you think Dad'll get pissed that you're showing off, even though you're not. And if you get them wrong, you think Dad'll be happy because he thinks that you think you're a know-it-all. Do I have this about right?"

Nothing.

"I'll take that as a yes."

Nothing.

"Now. Dad, does it bother you when I shout them out?"

"No."

"And I've gotten quite a few wrong. Does that make you feel good?"

"No."

"Would it bother you if Mom shouted them out?"

Nothing.

"Would you be happy if she kept getting them wrong?"

Nothing.

"What are you trying to start?" Mom was getting angry.

"I'm trying to stop you two from acting so silly! You . . . are . . . not . . . at . . . war! It's not *High Noon*. It's just a game, and if you stopped trying to psychoanalyze each other, you might be able to have a little fun."

The next time we watched "Jeopardy" together, Mom and I shouted out answers. And Dad didn't get mad. In fact, he bet me $10 I would blow the Final Jeopardy question.

"You got so damn many wrong, I think I have a good shot," he said.

I lost the bet. Mom laughed.

The Cold War between Mom and Dad did not end, but détente started.

Dear Father,

Enclosed are two round-trip tickets from Los Angeles to Cleveland. One is for you, and the other for Mom. The tickets are non-refundable.

You will be staying with me for eight days. I know you hate to shut down the restaurant to take vacation. But I also know you hate even more the thought of my losing the money I paid for the tickets.

See you next month on the 7th. Bring your blue suit. Have Mom pick out a tie.

Did I mention that the tickets are non-refundable?

Love,

Your son.

I knew that if I mailed them two round-trip tickets to Cleveland, Mom and Dad would come—as long as the tickets were non-refundable.

Oh, Dad moaned about how he couldn't take off from the restaurant, and Mom made a bunch of excuses because she really didn't want to travel with him. But they came. I knew they would.

The city is beautiful in the fall. Cleveland sunsets overlooking

Lake Erie are spectacular. Every color is painted in the sky—deep red, purple, orange, yellow, green, and all the in-betweens—as if an artist were mad at his canvas. Yes, it's cool to knock the city. But as a friend and native Clevelander put it, it's a "whelming" city—not underwhelming, not overwhelming, but "whelming."

I took Mom and Dad to the Cleveland Museum. We watched the Cleveland Indians lose. They met my friends. They visited Thurman.

"Hey, partner," Dad said.

"Got a light?" Thurman said. He told his wife and my mom about having stolen and lost Dad's cigarette case and holder all those years ago.

As my mom and aunt talked in the kitchen, Dad and Thurman talked for hours in the living room. They talked about Chattanooga and Uncle Eddie. They laughed about how Dad pretended to be "the telephone man," and made Uncle Eddie set the phone down, back away six feet, and yell. Dad, relaxed and loose, acted just like Mom with Aunt Dorothy and her other friends.

That night, I took Mom and Dad to Benihana's. I knew Dad would get a kick out of the knife tossing and the cooking theatrics. They ordered shrimp, lobster, and steak—to Dad this was dining at its finest.

"You know, I figured out why your marriage had so much friction."

They stopped eating and looked up.

"Dad, you wanted a woman just like Aunt Juanita, didn't you?"

He paused. "Probably."

"And Mom, you wanted a man like—Dirty Harry."

They roared.

"No, Larry," she said, "Dirty Harry is a wimp."

I have a photo from that night. I keep it on my desk, right next to the little black-and-white one of the café. And next to them, the note that Dad sent me after The Talk.

That week in Cleveland, Mom and Dad slept in my bed. As I got up one morning to get them coffee, I thought I heard something—something strange. They were in bed, awake, sitting up. Talking.

23

KIRK AND DAD

I called Kirk. "Are you up for dinner? I'm buying."

Kirk and I never spent time together as adults. He joined the Navy when he was eighteen. I was fifteen. He was assigned to the Sixth Fleet. I went off to college, and didn't return to L.A. for years. When he got out, he went back to L.A. and tried to work with Dad.

It had been twenty-five years since Kirk and I lived under the same roof or even in the same city. Lots of things had happened in that period of time, and we were awkwardly beginning to get into a kind of sync. We always got along growing up, about as well as brothers can with a three-and-a-half year age gap.

Kirk was a bad-ass athlete back in those days. He was big and strong, with amazing hand-eye coordination. When we played on playgrounds or in pick-up games with neighborhood kids, Kirk excelled.

In Little League, Kirk pitched for a team called the Dodgers. I played for the Cubs. My first year of Little League, the Dodgers and Cubs were scheduled to play each other twice, late in the season.

Kirk was the Dodgers' starting pitcher, and had won all his

games so far that season. This would be our first time facing each other for real, in a game that mattered. We were washing dishes the night before. I was dreading our face-off. David had better odds against Goliath. I figured Kirk would fire the ball, and I'd wave my bat three times—if I was lucky—and it would be back to the bench. Couldn't Kirk ease up on the fastball just a little so I wouldn't embarrass myself?

"I don't know about that," he said.

"I can't hit and you know it. I just don't want to look stupid."

Kirk knew I was an easy out, and allowing me to at least make contact wouldn't really hurt his team. But he felt uncomfortable.

"Why don't we ask Dad?" he said.

Dad? We never asked Dad anything. Not advice on how to deal with bullies. Not advice on what to do when we liked a girl. Not advice on homework. Dad came home angry, sat down angry, ate dinner angry, and watched television angry. Then we cleared a path for him when he walked down the hall to go to bed.

I wasn't sure Dad cared or even knew much about baseball— other than he thought going to the ballpark was a pain.

"I don't know about asking him."

"Yeah," Kirk said, "me neither."

"Do you guys want somethin'?" Dad had overheard us. We thought he'd been sleeping in his green chair. "Well, what is it?"

Kirk explained our dilemma—that I couldn't hit his pitches, but he didn't want to make me look stupid. At least, not too stupid.

"Let me tell you somethin'." Dad turned off the television. "Kirk, your job is to blow that ball right by him. You won't be doin' him any favors by slackin' off. Your job, Larry, is to try and tear the cover off the ball. You won't get any better if you don't. And whatever happens, happens. You got to be prepared in life. If you're not prepared, one of two things will happen. Do you know what they are?"

"No."

"You goin' to get your ass kicked, or your feelin's hurt."

The next morning, Saturday, Dad went to his first—and last—Little League game. I ripped Kirk—a triple, a double, and two singles. The Cubs beat the Dodgers 13–6. The second game that season was the same result. I hit three doubles and the Cubs defeated the Dodgers 12–5.

Kirk and I laughed about those games while we ate dinner.

"You need to fix things with Dad," I said.

"Why?"

"Just sit down with him and hear him out."

"Why?"

"There's a reason why he is the way he is."

"There's a reason why everybody is the way they are."

Dad made me stubborn and determined. He made Kirk the same way. After he left the restaurant, Kirk started working for an oil company in a refinery. Hard working and likeable, he was given more and more responsibility. After a few years, he made foreman with even brighter prospects down the road. He married a woman with two children, and they had another. He is happy. He complains sometimes about money, but not often.

Because of Dad, he told me, he always wanted a family where the kids respected but actually liked their father. He intended to be the anti-Dad Dad.

When it came to Dad, Kirk made peace with there being no peace between them.

"You don't know how long we're going to have him," I said. "If he dies and you haven't tried, you're going to have to live with that the rest of your life."

"I've lived with it so far."

When Kirk would visit their house, he spoke only to Mom. Dad would get "How about those Dodgers?" "I don't know about the Lakers this year," or, "It looks like rain." And Dad would grunt back a couple of syllables.

"Kirk, I just think you should try." I said.

"You could talk a monkey out of his last peanut. But stay out of this."

"Larry, have you talked to your brother?" Dad asked me a few weeks later. He never asked me about Kirk.

"No, about what?"

"Anythin'."

"Why?"

"Well, he called and said he wanted to come over and talk."

"Really?"

"Yeah."

"And?"

"We had a long talk, the longest talk we ever had. And I was just wonderin' if he said anythin' to you."

"No, he hasn't."

"Hm-m-m. Well, we had a long talk. Kind of cleared the air."

"That's good, Dad."

"Yeah, it was. It really was. And you hadn't talked to him."

"No, sure haven't."

"Well, I'll say."

Dad asked me to help him clean out the garage.

"Time to get rid of all this useless old stuff."

I found an envelope in the bottom of a trunk. It was a letter that my dad, at age thirty-six, wrote to my older brother. Dad wrote it because he had a premonition that he would die at the age of thirty-six.

"Why thirty-six?" I asked.

"I don't know, but that's how long I thought I'd live."

"Well, you didn't exactly nail that prediction."

He said he wanted to leave a list of the life lessons learned, to help my brother who was then two years old. He wanted Kirk to have a "road map."

I framed the original and gave it to my brother. A copy hangs on my living room wall.

May 4, 1951

Kirk, my son, you are now starting out in life—a life that Mother and I cannot live for you.

So as you journey through life, remember it's yours, so make it a good one. Always try to cheer up the other fellow.

Learn to think straight, analyze things, be sure you have all the facts before concluding, and always spend less than you earn.

Make friends, work hard, and play hard. Most important of all remember this—the best of friends wear out if you use them.

This may sound silly, Son, but no matter where you are on the 29th of September, see that Mother gets a little gift, if possible, along with a big kiss and a broad smile.

When you are out on your own, listen and take advice but do your own thinking, and concluding, set up a reasonable goal, and then be determined to reach it. You can and will, it's up to you, Son.

Your Father,
Randolph Elder

24

DAD LIGHTENS UP

We watched the Olympic heavyweight weightlifting event. When the weight got up to around 580 pounds, nobody could lift it. The athletes grunted and groaned. Everyone dropped the bar. No one pulled off a clean and jerk. A big, bearded Russian was up.

"I think this guy has a shot," Dad said.

"Gee, I don't know. Nobody else has come even close."

"I got a good feelin' about this guy."

"I don't think so."

"Wanna bet?" he said.

"Okay, I'll take your money. $5?"

"Make it $20?"

"$20? You've never bet that much before. After I win, you might have to get a job to pay it off."

"I don't know. I'm feelin' lucky."

The Russian powdered his hands. Then he bent down, grabbed the bar, and hoisted it over his head—a clean and jerk! The crowed exploded. A new world record!

"Damn."

"Pay up, chump," he said.

I gave him a twenty. He rubbed it, snapped it a couple of times, and held it up to the light.

"Looks real."

About an hour later, I saw the *Los Angeles Times* sports page on his bed. On the front page was a big color picture of the Russian weightlifter hoisting the barbell with the record-breaking weight. The caption read: "New World Record." Dad and I had watched a tape-delayed event—whose outcome he'd read about that morning.

"You cheated."

"How so?"

"That was a tape."

"So?"

"You already knew he'd do it!"

"So?"

"So it's like you bet on a horse to win a race he'd already won."

"It's not my fault you didn't know it was taped."

"And you don't think you should have told me?"

"And lose out on $20?" he said. "What kind of chump do you take me for, chump?"

"You could at least have the dignity to say you didn't know it was taped."

"That'd be lyin'. I don't lie, chump."

Kirk and I told Dad about a big "fight" party we went to where they showed a live championship fight. They passed a hat around. You put in twenty dollars and picked out a number from one to twelve. If the fight ended in the round of your number, you won part of the pot.

One of the fighters was heavily favored to win, with experts predicting an early knockout, most likely in the third round.

"Hey, give me twenty bucks," Kirk said.

I gave him the money and he picked the third round. I put in my twenty and picked a most unlikely round, the tenth. Damn!

"C'mon, Kirk," I said. "Trade rounds with me."

"No."

"Hey, you wouldn't be playing at all if I hadn't given you the twenty."

He laughed. "Screw you."

As predicted, the favorite wailed on the underdog in the first and second rounds. But the favorite failed to put him away in the third, and the tide started turning.

By the middle rounds, it was clear that this was going to be a long night. By the seventh and eighth round, the momentum had shifted to the underdog. In the ninth round, the favorite was getting smacked around and barely made it back to his corner. Assuming the favorite answered the tenth round bell, he was finished. His cornerman frantically tried to get him ready to go back out.

Kirk leaned over, "Can we still trade rounds?"

"Screw you."

The favorite was knocked out in the tenth round. I won $240.

"I don't know what's scarier," Dad said. "That Kirk was stupid enough to ask you to trade. Or that you might have been stupid enough to do it. Either way, it's bad."

We were in the breakfast room eating watermelon. Dad methodically cut a large half-slice into tidy, medium-large bite-size squares.

"Why don't you scrape the seeds off before you put the watermelon in your mouth, like I do?"

"Takes too much time."

"Isn't it more trouble to spit out the seeds?"

"Not to me."

Dad put a piece in his mouth, chewed, and spit the seeds onto his fork.

"Do you know that you're swallowing seeds?"

"No, I'm not."

"Yes, you are."

"No, I'm not."

"That chunk you just put in your mouth, it had at least a half a dozen seeds—and those are just the ones I saw from my side."

"And?"

"When you spit out the seeds, only four came out. You are swallowing seeds."

"No, I'm not."

"Yes, you are."

"I've been eatin' watermelon all my life."

We counted the black seeds in the next chunk on his plate. There were eight visible on the outside, and maybe one or two more in deep, but eight at a minimum.

He put the piece in his mouth, bit down, chewed awhile, and starting spitting out the seeds onto his fork. We counted them.

"One. Two. Three. Four." That's it. He was done. No more seeds. He was shocked.

"Eight minus four means you swallowed four seeds."

"I'll be damned."

"So let's do the math. You've been eating watermelon all your life. We add up the number of watermelons per year, times the number of years you've been eating them and, let's see, that means you've probably swallowed over 100,000 watermelon seeds. That's a lot of seeds. I'm amazed you can even have a bowel movement."

"All right, you two," Mom said from next room. "That's sick."

Dad and I were watching the news: "Turning to Hollywood, Elizabeth Taylor has finalized her divorce from her last husband, making a total of eight divorces . . . "

"Dad, what do you think about that?"

"What do I think about what?"

"Elizabeth Taylor getting married and divorced eight times."

"I don't think anythin' about it."

"You have no opinion?"

"Larry, it isn't worth the energy to form one."

Dad and I were sitting at the dining room table when Mom came down the hall.

"I smell something burning," she said.

Dad didn't lift his head from his newspaper. "Maybe you're walkin' too fast."

One evening, my dad was in his chair watching the news as my mother sat on the couch mending something. The anchor talked about the latest man to join the craze of "streaking," running nude down a public street.

"You know," Dad said, "I'm thinkin' about takin' up streakin'."

Mom stared at the fabric and tugged on the needle. "You won't draw much of a crowd."

Dad now laughs all the time.

25

DAD'S NEW CAR

D ad loves cars. He used to identify the make, model, and year until "those damn foreign things" started "poppin up."

"Dad, would you like a new car?"

"For what?"

"To have a new car."

"Don't need one," he said. Long retired, he occasionally drove to the store or to his Spanish classes.

In 1955, he bought a green 1954 Mercury, our first "new" family car. He never bought a real new car. And he drove each car until it needed a root canal.

"Dad, you've never had a new car. I want you to have one. I want you to know what a new car smells like."

"Okay, if that's what you want."

"That's what I want."

"I don't want you takin' on no debt."

"I won't."

"The moment I feel too old to drive, that's the day you come get the car. Deal?"

"Deal."

He wanted a Ford. He went from car to car, asking about mileage, maintenance, and trade-in value before selecting a white Ford Taurus. We caravanned home. In my rearview window, I saw him smile all the way back home, looking happier than a kid with his first puppy. We both did.

He wouldn't park it in the driveway. He parked it in front of the house.

"That way I can look at it when I drink my coffee."

About a year later, an eighty-six-year-old man plowed into a bunch of shoppers at a busy outdoor farmers' market in Santa Monica. Instead of pressing the brake, he mashed the accelerator. He killed ten people, including a seven-month-old baby, and injured more than fifty. "It was crazy," one eyewitness said. "It was terrifying. There were bodies everywhere. He just kept accelerating. The screaming moved down the street in a wave."

Dad called me the day of the tragedy. "Come get this car."

"But you just passed your last driver's test."

"I don't care. Come get this car right now."

"Are you sure you don't want to think about it a little more? You're still driving fine."

"I don't care," he said, "I'm not goin' to let the same thing happen to me. Now, come get this car."

I took it back. It had less than eight hundred miles.

"It's the most beautiful car I ever had in my life," he said. "But it's better to quit too soon than to stay too long."

26

DAD AND FRIENDS— LOST AND GAINED

Aside from my Uncle Thurman in Cleveland, my father truly liked and respected only one other man—Mr. Lusk. Mr. and Mrs. Lusk moved next door about two or three years after we moved to Haas Avenue. They were originally from Texas, but had come to L.A. in the late '40s around the same time as my parents.

They had no children. Mrs. Lusk wore no-nonsense sweaters, took the bus to work, and canned her own peaches. Mr. Lusk kept a garden where he grew cabbage, green beans, and onions. They had a small peach tree and also grew berries. Everywhere in his small back yard where it was humanly possible to grow something edible, Mr. Lusk found a way.

Mr. Lusk reminded Dad of himself, and Mr. Lusk saw a mirror image in Dad. Both were Depression-era men. Both were no-nonsense, unpretentious, and direct. No excuses—life is what you make of it. No complaining—except when they complained about government, welfare, lazy people, and "good-for-nothin' kids who ain't got to do nothin' but go to school and they won't half do that." What are the odds of two such people—two loners with no other friends—in a city of three million people moving next door to each other?

Mrs. Lusk called her husband "Puddin." We used to joke about it until my dad told us to cut it out. Mrs. Lusk worked for the city as a clerk of some kind. She left every morning at the same time, and returned home at exactly the same time every evening. Mr. Lusk worked for the railroads, something to do with switching the tracks so the right railcars hooked up with the right engines.

The Lusks were frugal. They bought a new car only when the old one was on life support. Their home was sparsely furnished, and their garage neat, clean, and organized. They lived next door for some forty years.

"How ya doin', Mr. Lusk?" Dad said. The Lusks' first names were Fred and Arletha. But the Lusks called my parents "Mr. Elder" and "Mrs. Elder," and Mom and Dad called them "Mr. Lusk" and "Mrs. Lusk."

"Oh, can't complain. If I did you wouldn't listen."

"Well, 90 percent of people don't want to hear 'bout your problems, and the other 10 percent are glad it's you."

They'd laugh, exchange jokes, and complain about their wives. The wives retaliated and complained about their "good-for-nothin'" husbands.

Mr. Lusk joked about my mother's take-no-prisoners drive and referred to her as the "War Department." Once, after Mom was promoted to supervisor at the phone company, she forgot her reading glasses. The company sent a lower-level employee to our house to pick up her glasses. Mr. Lusk came unglued.

"So, War Department, you're such a big wheel, you had some flunky come out and get your glasses. Bet you left them on purpose."

And if Dad got home early enough, he'd grab some vodka,

open the Lusks' back gate, and invite himself in for a drink.

Mr. Lusk, an avid San Francisco Giants fan, loved baseball. I was never sure whether he was truly a Giants fan or whether he pretended just to annoy me. He taught me how to throw a curve ball. And even though our basketballs invariably went over the fence and crushed his onions, he never got mad.

"Now, you boys watch your ball," he said while tossing it back. "You're ruining my crop over here. So try and be careful."

Mr. Lusk retired first. Dad kept promising, "This is my last year." But he kept on working.

"This time," Dad said, "I mean it." He was eighty-one and said he was giving it one more year.

He and Mr. Lusk began planning the things they were going to do together. They would travel. They would maybe go fishing. They talked about taking in a Giants-Dodgers game. Most likely, though, they would just hang out and shoot the breeze.

This time Dad was serious. He asked me to sell the business and the house next to it.

"You take care of all the legal stuff. I assume you'll give me a discount."

"No, I'm charging extra—aggravation tax."

Four weeks before Dad retired, Mr. Lusk died. His stomach had suddenly swollen. He checked into a hospital and within days, he was dead. My father was devastated.

"Well, I'll be damned. I'll be damned." He would now have a very different retirement.

My friend, Donna, wanted me to meet her father who lived in Scottsdale, Arizona. Bill, her father, served in World War II on a combat ship and did some boxing in the Navy. When he came out, he worked as a metal spinner. He was tall, still muscular, with tattoos on each arm. He reminded me of John Wayne.

"You mean what John Wayne wished he was," said Donna.

"My Dad is the real deal." One day, she said, a bunch of young men were walking down his street drinking and yelling.

"Keep it down!" Bill barked.

"Mind your own business."

"This neighborhood is my business. Now keep it down or I'll come over there and kick your ass."

He was then over seventy.

"We gotta get them together," Donna said. "Your dad reminds me of mine."

When Bill and his wife, Carol, came to L.A., Donna arranged for Dad and Bill to meet.

"Now my dad is not much for small talk," I warned Donna.

Bill and Dad talked for two hours, told jokes, and drank vodka. When Carol stuck her head in to check on him, Bill shooed her away.

"I'm fine." Dad and Bill kept talking.

Bill called me later. "Meeting your Dad and hearing about his life is one of the greatest experiences I've ever had. Maybe your parents might want to drive to Scottsdale and stay with us. We have plenty of room."

"You want them to drive to Scottsdale and stay with you?" Mom and Dad, visiting new people, enclosed in the same car for hours, and then staying in a guest's home—in the same bed? Good luck with that.

"Okay," I said. "I'll ask."

They went.

Joyce, a family friend, drove. They stayed with Bill and Carol a week.

Bill used a "family pass" to take them to the Grand Canyon. The woman at the entrance looked at his pass, then looked at the posse of blacks and whites standing next to Bill.

"Sir, this pass is for your family."

"Right." Bill smiled, and wrapped his arms around Mom, Dad, Joyce, and Carole. "Here they are!"

"Ah, okay, sir. Have a good time."

Bill and Dad stayed in touch.

"Randolph," Mom would hand Dad the phone. "It's Bill again."

DAD AND DENNIS

My prediction that Dennis would kill or be killed turned out to not be entirely accurate.

Dennis tried to kill himself. He ingested rat poison.

Mom got a call in the middle of the night from a San Francisco hospital.

"Are you the mother of Dennis Elder?"

Someone found Dennis in a coma, passed out on a residential street. Through identification in his wallet, they traced him back to Mom and Dad.

When he regained consciousness, he said he wasn't really trying to kill himself. The woman he was living with threatened to put him out of her apartment. To stop her, he put rat poison in his food. He thought it would only make his stomach hurt. Then he'd go to the hospital and get his stomach pumped while she cried and held his hand. She'd see how much he loved her and would let him stay.

But the poison didn't work—at least not right away. He assumed it was old and no longer potent. Two days later, he was walking to the store and collapsed. His body started convulsing.

After that, he remembered nothing.

He recovered to a degree, but the poison ravaged his insides. His kidneys, heart, and even brain had been affected. The poison caused him to contract adult-onset diabetes, and it got progressively worse.

Dennis moved back to L.A., and bounced around while staying with this or that friend. He always managed to find a "friend" with a place for him to stay.

"Jesus, his life is less stressful than mine," I told Mom. "He finds more places to live than John Lesley." Even she laughed.

"Mom, I'm over at a friend's apartment on Slauson, would you bring me a carton of cigarettes?" he'd say.

And off she'd go in the car to a store in the middle of the night, to fetch smokes for her grown son. I was livid.

"You don't have compassion," she said.

Eventually, I stopped arguing with her about Dennis. What's more potent than a mother's love for her child? I remembered the hen at Grandma's farm that almost blinded me in defense of her little chick.

Dennis met his future wife. Shortly after their marriage, they moved to Arizona, her home state. "Great," I thought, "the further away from Mom the better. No more late-night phone calls."

After his suicide attempt, the doctors told us that Dennis, then childless, would be impotent. "A blessing in disguise," I thought. "He's too irresponsible to bring kids into this world." He proceeded to have three, plus two stepchildren he inherited when he married.

Then he and his wife separated, but stayed in touch. When Dennis moved backed to L.A., his children visited constantly, usually staying at Mom and Dad's.

Dennis, for years, was in and out of hospitals. Even when I came to see him, we argued. I went to visit at him at General, the same hospital where he was born. Another 9-1-1 by some friend, and another stay at a hospital where Mom would pace the halls and wait for the doctor to tell her he would be all right.

I asked a floor nurse for directions to his room.

"Are you Mr. Dennis's brother?" asked the shy Filipina nurse. "Hey, everybody, this is Mr. Dennis's brother."

She lowered her voice and looked around as if she might get into trouble.

"Could you get him to stop cursing? We try to do our best for Mr. Dennis. But he just, you know, screams and yells."

Three other women nodded.

"I'll talk to him."

He was sitting up watching television, flipping through channels with the remote.

"Nothing on television. No cable. Some hospital."

"I'll talk to the CEO about upgrading your accommodations." Stop it, I told myself.

"You don't have to be sarcastic."

"You don't have to act like this is the Four Seasons."

"This guy is sick," I thought. "He can't help acting this way, but you can. So calm down."

We talked a bit about Mom and Dad and how worried they were about him.

"You know, Dennis," I said at what I felt was a good time. "I don't know how long you're going to be here, but the nurse wants you to stop screaming—"

"Those bitches. They won't tell you anything! I asked what time I was gonna eat, and they wouldn't tell me! Why am I taking this shot? Won't tell me. How long am I going to be here? Wouldn't tell me. I'm not an animal. I deserve to know what's going on! At least tell me when I'm going to eat, Goddammit!"

"That's right, Dennis. These nurses get up in the morning

and say, 'What can I do to make Dennis Elder's life miserable?'"

"I just want them to answer my questions! Is that too much to ask?"

"If you treated the nurses better, maybe they'd tell you what you want to know."

"If they told me what I wanted to know, maybe I'd treat them better."

"So you're admitting you treat them like crap?"

"I'm not admitting anything."

"You just did."

"No I didn't."

"Why did I even bother coming?"

"Good question."

"Would you rather I leave?"

"Suit yourself."

"Give me strength," I thought. "He's lying in the hospital, getting weaker and weaker, and still we argue. What's wrong with him? What's wrong with me?"

The nurse stuck her head in the door. Her expression said, "Well?"

"I talked to him."

"Oh, thank you. And, Mr. Dennis, we'll be feeding you at 5 o'clock."

I turned to Dennis. "See?"

"See, nothing. She should have said that in the first place."

Four months later, he died.

Mom insisted on holding the funeral at a large church.

"We need a place big enough for all his friends," she said.

A large church? Honestly? Dennis's "friends" seemed to pop up when he had money, and disappear when he was out. They are the kind who change addresses all the time, unstable, always moving, living-on-the-edge-of-life folks you can't exactly locate and notify by phone.

"The number you have dialed is no longer in service." I called five phone numbers I'd scrounged up and I got five of those recordings.

We managed to track down and tell a few people about the services, and told a few neighbors and a couple of other people who knew him, and that was that. We didn't put a notice in the paper—and if we had, who among his acquaintances would have read it? Even if they had, so what? It's not like they were going to drop everything and come to his funeral.

"No," said Mom, rejecting the suggestion of a much smaller church for the funeral. "Dennis has lots of friends. They'll be there."

Neither Dad nor I wanted to speak at Dennis's funeral—Dad because he just doesn't speak in public, and me because I wasn't going to say some insincere things about what a great guy he was. Mom couldn't speak because she wouldn't have been able to control herself.

Dad lost weight and looked fifteen pounds lighter than only a few days earlier. Mom said he just stopped eating. At the funeral, he stared straight ahead, occasionally shaking someone's hand.

So Kirk spoke for the family.

Kirk told funny stories about Dennis, pranks they pulled on each other, the time they spent in Arizona.

"And he absolutely loved his children," Kirk said. "And we're going to miss him."

Kirk sat down and he whispered, "Can you believe all these people?"

His children and his ex-wife were at the funeral. And they cried when Mom's pastor spoke about him.

So many others came, too. People from our elementary school. People he met in junior high school. People from Crenshaw High, and not just from Dennis's class.

Former neighbors, some I last saw twenty or thirty years ago, came up to Mom and Dad. Many cried, telling Mom and Dad them how much they loved Dennis. Even the "low-lifes and thugs" came, several driving in from Arizona.

I saw faces I barely remembered, others I had completely forgotten about. Men and women—who I knew as little boys and girls—told my mother how much they liked him, how funny he was, and then told of his many acts of friendship and kindness. Several referred to him as "Chico," a nickname somebody gave him in high school for who knows why.

"Are you Chico's brother?" one said. "He talked about you all the time."

He did?

"Someone said you are Chico's older brother?"

"I'm one of them," I said.

"The one on the radio? He never missed your show. Used to point to the radio and say, 'You know who that is?'"

He did?

"Used to say, 'He could be president someday, but I think he's too smart to do that.' And I laughed and Chico said, 'I'm serious as a heart attack.'"

"Would anyone now like to come up and say a few words about this man who touched so many lives?" the pastor asked.

A line formed. As one speaker sat down, another took his place in line. Some dressed in suits, others in dress pants and shirts, many wore jeans, and some looked as if they borrowed something, anything, to try and look appropriate.

"I don't know how he did it," one said, "but Chico put up the money to bail me out."

"Me and Chico used to go out of town together to visit my Mom in Henderson," another said.

"We used to sit up all night and play cards, and I'll tell you what, he could tell jokes."

"If Chico had money, he'd say, 'Let's go and get a brew,' and never asked for pay back."

"He lived next door to me in Phoenix, and would give me advice on what to do about that crazy husband I used to have. Whenever he went to the store, he asked me if I needed anything. And . . . ." The woman broke down. Another mourner retrieved her and helped her back to her seat.

"He used to give me advice," said a man in his early twenties, one of dozens of people I had never seen and knew nothing about.

One told stories of a stray cat he found and cared for.

All but one of his children briefly spoke, the youngest too distraught to say anything. Mom was right. People came.

After Dennis's funeral, for whatever reason, Dad never again said, "I wish I had known. Maybe I could've done somethin'."

· 28 ·

DAD NEVER LEARNED
TO HATE

A few years after I started on radio in L.A., "60 Minutes" interviewed me. They wanted to know about how my parents shaped my thinking, so they came out to their house. The crew set up lights, sound, cameras, and had professionals put on make-up. Mom was interviewed first. She talked about my career, about how she felt about those who attacked me and whether it affected her emotionally. Dad sat in a chair in the corner the whole time they were setting up and during Mom's interview. Then it was his turn.

Morley Safer sat across from him. Safer talked to Dad about his hard life in the country, during the Depression and Jim Crow.

Mr. Elder, said Safer, your son says if you work hard, keep your nose clean, you can make it in life. Is that how you feel?

"Worked for me," Dad said. "Worked for me."

When the piece aired, the only part of Dad's interview they used was, "Worked for me, worked for me."

Dear Larry,

I've listened to you for years, but only recently found out that you are the son of the man who ran Elder's Snack Bar on Valencia Street.

Tell your father that the food was amazing, especially the biscuits and pancakes.

I used to work at Jeffries Banknotes, not far from the restaurant. Everybody who worked there ate at your Dad's place.

Please say hello to him for me. (Tell him I'm the one he used to tease for wearing the San Francisco Giants baseball cap.)

Sergio

I've received dozens of letters like this one. Dad's response is always the same.

"I just did my best."

I brought my parents to hear one of my speeches. I talked about my appreciation for my mother and of how her influence made me believe in myself.

Then I talked about my dad's life:

I have been accused of—I'll try to put this in as nice a way as possible—"naiveté" for my feeling that this country, with all of its flaws, is the fairest, most decent country in history. And I want to tell you a little bit about why I feel that way. I want to tell you a story about two Americans—one not so famous, the other, infamous. They're both roughly the same age, grew up in the same era, both grew up in the same area of the South.

The first, not so famous, is a black man. He is now eighty-two years old, and grew up in Athens, Georgia. Until he was five years old, he assumed that the woman who raised him was his mother, only to later be informed it was not his mother; it was his grandmother. He never knew his father. His real mother, who later raised him, had a series of—let's call them "friends"—one of whom used to beat her regularly. Once his mother wanted to attend her own mother's funeral and the man didn't want her to go. He beat her so badly she was bedridden and missed her own mother's funeral.

This boy grew up in this family and, when he was thirteen years old, he came home one day and was making too much noise for the mother's "friend." The mother's friend got angry and the mother sided with her boyfriend. He was basically thrown out of the house at the age of thirteen. He then went down the street, hearing taunts from the mother, "You'll be back, and if you won't be back, you'll be in the penitentiary soon." He walked down the street and was taken in by a white family, where he began to cook for them. He did that for a time, and then began a series of jobs: shoeshine boy, bellhop. He decided to apply for a job as a Pullman porter—at the time Pullman was the largest private employer of blacks in the country. He got a job, traveled around the country for the first time, including California. World War II broke out; he became a private, ultimately a sergeant, stationed in Guam. And he was a cook—cooked for thousands and thousands of GIs during the Second World War.

When the war was over, he returned to the South where he wanted to get a job as a short-order cook, and he was told that he had no references, even though he had cooked for thousands of people during the nation's war effort against Nazi Germany, Fascist Italy, and Imperialist Japan.

He decided after he got married he would go out to California, a place where he had visited as a Pullman porter, because it seemed so fresh and sunny and open and liberal. So he came out in the '40s, and applied to a series of places to get a job as a cook, and was told he had no references. So he went to an unemployment office and sat and sat and sat, and finally got a job as a janitor, worked at that place for a number of years, while simultaneously working at another place as a janitor, and he cooked for a private family on the weekends, and attended night school to get his G.E.D.—he had always felt inadequate and insecure because he didn't have a high school diploma.

Meanwhile, he and his wife have three children. He later saves enough money to start a restaurant—he is now in his early forties—and he successfully ran this restaurant for thirty years near downtown Los Angeles.

A tougher life I have rarely come across. Yet he never hated, he was never bitter, he never condemned his circumstances, and he always said there are very few problems that cannot be solved through hard work.

The man I speak of is my father.

The other man, who grew up in the same era, in the same geographical area, and is the same age, is famous. He became governor of Alabama, and in an unforgettable statement, said, "Segregation now, segregation tomorrow, segregation forever." He stood in the doorway and prevented black students from attending the University of Alabama. He personified the bigoted, Jim Crow, segregationist South.

He ran for president, and was shot—paralyzed from the waist down. For the first time, he began to understand what it was like to be helpless, began to understand what it must be like to be black. At the end of his career, he began to reflect on his past, and he showed up unannounced in 1978 at the Dexter Avenue Baptist Church in Montgomery, Alabama—you might be familiar with that church. It's the church from which one Martin Luther King Jr. became the spiritual head of the modern civil rights movement. At the time, there were three hundred black ministers and lay leaders of Alabama churches conducting a day-long conference. Mr. Wallace was wheeled in unexpectedly and asked to speak to the gathering. They allowed him to speak and he said, and I quote, "I never had hate in my heart for any person, but I regret my support of segregation, and the pain it caused the black people of our state and our nation."

Amid cries of "Amen" and "Yes, Lord," Mr. Wallace added, and I quote, "I've learned what pain is, and I'm sorry if I caused anybody else pain. Segregation was wrong, and I am sorry."

Two men—one not so famous, one infamous. One never learned to hate, and one finally learned to stop.

If Mr. Wallace can be forgiven, then America can be forgiven, and that's why, ladies and gentlemen, I have hope for this country.

Then I introduced Mom and Dad to the crowd.

They received a standing ovation—a standing ovation for a southern woman with a year of college and her husband, an "outside" child from an illiterate mother. They stood and smiled and waved.

I leaned over to Dad during the thunderous applause. "What did you think?"

"Big fuss over nothin'," he said. "Just did the best I could."

The following day, I took Dad to see a movie. He made me assure him that we would, absolutely, positively, at all times, sit near an exit close to the bathroom—"just in case."

I chose *Sling Blade* for no particular reason—I'd just heard good things. It was about a mentally disturbed man confined to a psychiatric institution since the then-boy murdered his mother and her lover. Released, he finds a job, and befriends a child. He learns that the boy lives in fear of his mom's boyfriend, an evil, physically violent man who threatens the mother and terrifies her son.

"I have to go," Dad leaned over and whispered in my ear.

"Okay, the bathroom is over here."

"No, I have to go home."

"Why?"

"Can't take this movie anymore."

"What's wrong?"

"This reminds me of how my daddy treated me."

We left. For the second time in my life, I saw him cry.

· 29 ·

CARRYING ON

"Come over right now!" Dad called frantically one morning. "They took your mother to the hospital!"

She was diabetic and had long been taking insulin injections. She was always careful, took her mediations on time, and constantly watched her diet. But she had fainted that morning.

The doctor and nurses tried to resuscitate her. I watched this strong, tough woman now connected to tubes, the doctor pumping her chest, and the other assistants scrambling around. Still, she grew weaker.

"Does she have a living will?" the doctor asked.

"Yes," I said.

"You should get it."

Less than an hour later, she seemed to stop breathing. She had taken the decision out of our hands—exactly the way she wanted. She was eighty-two.

"Whatever you do," she always told us, "do not let me live without my senses." She cringed when she watched the news about someone kept alive through "heroic measures."

"There's nothing heroic about being brain dead."

She was deeply disturbed about the Terry Schiavo case. Schiavo's husband insisted that she did not want to be kept on life support, while her parents insisted that she would never say such a thing. There was nothing in writing to settle the matter.

"Please do not let me stay alive in that condition," Mom said.

She and my father took out living wills, ensuring that any such decision would be made in accordance with her wishes. Dad just went along. "Whatever you say."

"There's nothing more we can do," the doctor said. "I'm sorry."

"Now what?" I said.

"There's nothing, there's . . . I'm sorry. We did all we could do. I'm, I'm sorry."

The doctor thought I refused to accept that she had died, and that I wanted his team to continue trying to save her.

"No, I'm sorry. I meant what happens next to her body? I mean, where do you place her? How does it work?"

"Oh. We have storage downstairs where we keep her for a few days while you make arrangements. The funeral home you choose will contact us, and pick her up."

"I see. Thank you."

I never made arrangements before, and never really thought about what to do. I just planned on Mom and Dad living forever.

"Jesus, Larry," Kirk said when the doctor walked away. "What happens next?"

My mother was almost ten years younger than my Dad. I expected him to go first. I knew that someday I would write about him, so I taped him for hours as he answered questions about his past, his hopes, his expectations, and his disappointments. I intended to do the same with my mother. I just assumed that there would be time. Time ran out.

Mom appeared on my radio show for years every Friday from

5 p.m. until 6 p.m. To Mr. Lusk, she was the "War Department." To her listeners, she was the "Chief Justice of the Supreme Court," with an answer for everything. Illegal immigration? "The United States should invade Mexico, develop it, and the country would be so prosperous the Mexicans would rather stay home." Government welfare? "Nothing for the able-bodied and able-minded, and as for everybody else, that's what churches are for." Global warming? "Just some crap made up so that Al Gore can get rich."

On Thursdays, she did movie reviews. *Basic Instinct 2*, with Sharon Stone? "Don't ever ask me to see a movie with all that sex, I'm not interested in watching sex, I already know how to do it and don't need to see it." *Brokeback Mountain*? "I didn't think I would like it, but it was a love story." *The 40-Year-Old Virgin*? "Hysterical, but I don't know why all his friends thought it was so important for him to lose his virginity—he was better adjusted than his friends."

Our show that last Friday was one of our best. She was blunt, irreverent, and funny in the at-this-stage-of-my-life-I-don't-give-a-damn-what-you-think way. Tatiana, a truck driver from South Carolina, called in. She wanted Mom to know how much she enjoyed hearing her on Fridays.

"Larry, your Mom is not just your mom. She America's Mom."

My mother and I laughed about the comment all weekend. On Tuesday morning, she was dead. My brother and I made funeral arrangements.

"What shall we put on it?" Kirk asked when we chose a headstone.

I told him about Tatiana's call.

"That's it, then, 'America's Mom.'"

My brother and I agreed that for all of Dad's complaining, he really had little idea of how much he not only depended upon her, but how much, in his way, he enjoyed her company. The

arguing, I finally realized, was their dance. It was their relationship. They had been at it for fifty-six years, and pretty much had
the routine down. She snapped. He snapped. She snapped back.
He snapped back, and at some point, the issue ran out of gas until
a new one came along. She fed him, washed his clothes, kept his
appointments, and breathed the same air.

And now she was gone.

"He won't last long without her," I told my brother.

She had a large funeral. In addition to her many friends from
our neighborhood, her church, and people she knew personally,
a bunch of her Friday afternoon radio fans came.

For the funeral, my brother and I had a black-and-white
photograph of her enlarged and put on display. She looked
wonderful, cheerful, with that don't-even-think-about-it sparkle
that said, "I know what I'm doing and how to do it so don't even
dream about trying to stop me." I brought the photo back to the
house. When I opened a closet to put it away, Dad stopped me.

"I'd like that put on the wall."

"Really? Where?"

"Where I can see it."

We decided to put it in her sewing room. Kirk and I secured
it to the wall, stepped back to see if it was hung evenly, and turned
to make sure it met with his approval.

She was no longer on her computer where she had taken to
emailing her fans, or on the phone making plans to go fabric
shopping with a friend, or giving me fifteen minutes of the latest
things Dad had done to annoy her.

"What do I do now?" Dad asked.

"You carry on, Dad," I said.

"For what?"

We looked around the sewing room—the room Kirk briefly
called his bedroom, where he'd once tacked pictures of Elvis on

the wall. We looked at her sewing machine and her last unfin-
ished project, a yellow jacket whose buttons were all that was left
to do. We looked at the pinking shears she kept just to her left,
next to the pin sponge, the spools of thread all neatly arranged
and color-coded. On a board above the sewing machine, she
nailed jar lids and screwed in the glass bottoms. She filled the
jars with buttons of various sizes, shapes, and colors. When a
button popped off one of Dad's shirts, she always found one
that was at least "close enough." We looked at her little television
set, the one she retreated to when she didn't like what Dad was
watching "up front."

"You're father's up front watching stand-up comedy," she'd say.

We looked at the picture we had just hung. And then Dad
reached for our hands. In their fifty-six year marriage, from the
time I entered the picture, I'd never seen him hold her hand. And
now he was holding ours—right in front of her picture.

He was crying. It was the third and last time I saw him cry.

How often does one spouse die only to be followed in death
a few days, weeks, or months by the surviving spouse? And the
husband is far more dependent on the wife than the other way
around, especially in a vintage 1940s marriage like this one.

"I don't know what I'm goin' to do," Dad said over and over.
We didn't know what else to say, but "carry on."

He says that he dreams about her every night. And he speaks
far more kindly of her than he ever did when she was alive. For a
while, he insisted that he didn't want to live, that he was a burden
on his children and his daughter-in-law.

But after a few months, he no longer insisted that life had no
meaning. Until recently he took walks, listened to his Spanish-
English language tapes, puttered around in the garden, and tried
to do a little housework.

I bring him obituary columns. He likes to hear about the

person's life, achievements, and the kind of legacy he or she left behind. He pretends not to, but he gets a kick out of hearing about people who died ten, fifteen, twenty years younger.

"Sounds like a nice life," he'll say when we read about someone's life. "He sure squeezed a lot in."

"So have you, Dad."

"She was eighty-three," he'd say. Or, "He was only seventy-nine." Or, "He was ninety-four."

"You beat 'em all, Dad." I say. "And you're still rocking."

"Ain't how long you lived. It's what you did with it."

30

"THINGS FALLIN' APART"

H e's become forgetful and complains "everythin' on me is fallin' apart."
"What is that you're holdin'?" Dad asked for the fifth time.

"It's an iPhone."

"What does it do?"

"It's a small computer so I can search for information." I showed him. "I can retrieve and send e-mail." I showed him. "I can use it for directions, to calculate, to store and play music, to write down appointments, to take notes, to use as a tape recorder, to take and store pictures." I showed him again.

"You say it's called an iPhone. Is it a phone, too?"

"Oh, yeah. It's a phone, too."

"Does all those things?"

"And more."

"Kind of like a Swiss Army knife."

"Yeah, kind of like that."

"Well, I'll say."

When he complains about his memory, I tell him there's an

upside.

"Really? What?"

"I can tell you the same jokes."

He's frustrated not to be able to follow the plots of movies. I suggested we watch older ones on the Turner Classic Movie channel. One night featured Paul Newman. We watched *The Sting, Cool Hand Luke, Paris Blues*, and *Rachel Rachel*. The marathon started at 7:15, about the time he goes to bed. But he watched every movie, and never fell asleep.

He especially enjoyed *Paris Blues*.

He lit up when he heard the opening music. "I haven't heard that in a long time. 'Take the A-Train,'" he said. "Duke Ellington."

I recognized a famous jazz piece.

"What's that called? What that called?" I muttered.

"Mood Indigo," he said.

"Oh."

We talked about the entertainers he enjoyed, the ones he told us about when we were kids. The Nicholas Brothers. Cab Calloway. Bill "Bojangles" Robinson. "Peg Leg" Bates, the dancer with the wooden leg. Each time, I pulled up the performer on YouTube with my iPhone.

"What's this thing called?"

"It's called an iPhone."

"And you can ask it to show these people?"

"Yes."

"Don't have to pay nothin'?"

"Nothing extra."

"It's a phone, too?"

"Yes. Does lots of things. Kind of like a Swiss Army knife."

"Well, I'll say."

31

"GOODNIGHT"

We watched a movie called *Proud*, about the true-life World War II experience of black sailors aboard the USS Mason. The ship was one of only two black-manned ships that actually saw combat. As a destroyer, it led Allied convoys through waters filled with German subs, and took on missions even the vaunted English Navy considered too treacherous. But the black sailors welcomed the assignments. They wanted to prove themselves in actual combat rather than the "menial" labor done by most blacks in the military of my father's era.

"I always thought that whole thing was stupid," Dad said.

"What whole thing?"

"Blacks wantin' to be on the front line, gettin' killed. If white people are so stupid they want to keep us in the back where it's safe, hell, let 'em. When all those civil rights people were sayin', 'Let us fight. Let us fight,' I'd say, 'Shut up, fool. They want to die, let 'em die.'"

A German sub launched a torpedo. But the blacks, thought too dumb to master hi-tech equipment like sonar detection, skillfully avoided getting hit. Then they counter-attacked with depth charges.

Despite their heroics, the men of the Mason never received a commendation. Their commander sent a letter to Washington urging recognition for these brave sailors. No dice.

After years of lobbying by the grandson of one of the sailors featured in the movie, President Clinton honored the surviving crewmen with a long-overdue ceremony. The USS Mason crew finally received their rightful commendation for bravery and sacrifice.

I watched my dad during the movie. As usual, his facial expression gave nothing away. What was he thinking? Was he thinking about his service as a staff sergeant and a cook? Was he thinking about Guam, where he and other soldiers prepared to assault Japan—a mission aborted because of Hiroshima and Nagasaki? Maybe he was just hungry for something to eat?

"Dad, what are you thinking about?"

He said the movie reminded him of something he hadn't really thought about in a long time.

"We had just gone through trainin' at Montford Point [in North Carolina]. We lined up to hear a speech—supposed to lift us up—that was given by a white major. I think that was his rank. The officer said, 'You know, I've traveled all over the world. But it only just now dawned on me that we are really at war. Because I came home and looked out, and saw you people wearin' our uniforms.'"

"Everybody was insulted. 'You people wearin' our uniforms'?"

Each black Marine just stood still, he said, a kind of silent protest against the officer's demeaning, racist statement. They remained standing when the officer left the podium and walked off the stage.

"'You people wearin' our uniforms.' What did that mean?"

Dad said. "Bet my ancestors beat his here."

I asked him about his training. He said it was rigorous and demanding, but that he expected it to be. And he was determined to do his duty.

"Montford Point?" I said, "I think there's a book about where you had your training."

I found it, ordered it online and showed it him: *The Marines of Montford Point: America's First Black Marines* by Melton Alonza McLaurin.

"Well, I'll say."

Reading and concentrating is now almost impossible. So I read some of the book to him each night as he lays in bed. He remembers some of the locations and activities described, but he either didn't know any of the men mentioned or can't remember them.

"It was a long, long time ago."

"There's a Montford Point group that stays in touch with each other online. Why don't I contact them?"

"No, that's okay."

"Don't you think might be fun to talk to some of the men you served with, see what they're up to?"

"No, that's okay. I know what I did. I know what they did. Now is now. Would you just turn out the light for me?"

"Right now?"

"If you don't mind. I'm feelin' a little tired. I just want to rest."

Tired, this man of steel? I thought of the time I first realized that he wouldn't be that way forever. Mom struggled to remove the top from a grape jar. She handed the jar to Dad, who couldn't unscrew the top either. Mom took the jar out of Dad's hands, and handed it to Kirk, who was then fifteen. Pop! I was astonished.

"How did you know Kirk could get it off?" I asked.

"Your father's strength is declining," she said. "Your brother is getting stronger. That's life."

That was a long time ago.

Dad pulls the covers up to his chin. I turn off the lamp. He smiles when I kiss him goodnight.

"I love you, Dad."

The light from the hallway touches his face. His skin is smooth and soft.

· ACKNOWLEDGMENTS ·

Once again, I want to thank my tireless, talented assistant, Dana Riley. This is our fourth outing.

And my thanks go to the wonderful people at WND Books. They immediately embraced this book and were a joy to work with.

I also want to thank several friends who read early versions of the manuscript and urged me to stay the course: Patricia Stewart and her mother, Mary, Burt Boyar, Stephen Sachs, Edgar Galindo, and Nina Perry. And, of course, my most important critic -- my brother, Kirk, who reassured me that that, yes, I had "gotten it right."

And finally, I cannot thank my best friend, Will Huhn, enough for his love, support, and encouragement.